5/30

Seventeenth-Century Painting

2616

Compass History of Art

Edited by André Held and D. W. Bloemena

The complete series includes:

Seventeenth-Century Painting

Raymond Cogniat

THE VIKING PRESS
New York

© 1964 by J. M. Meulenhoff Amsterdam
English translation © 1964 by George Weidenfeld and Nicolson Ltd
Photographs © 1964 by André Held
Translated by Frances Partridge

A COMPASS BOOKS original edition
Published in 1964 by The Viking Press, Inc.
625 Madison Avenue, New York, N.Y. 10022

Library of Congress catalog card number: 63–15219
Printed in Holland

Contents

Seventeenth-Century Painting

Introduction

The seventeenth century was the age when man proudly came into his own and, with new confidence in his own powers, began to impose his will and to examine and measure the forces which had hitherto mastered him. The twentieth century can be seen as the apotheosis of this state of things, for the ever-increasing sum of our knowledge gives the impression that our discoveries have gone beyond what our intelligence predicted. But this very excess has caused man to lose some of his primacy; he has become an infinitely small ingredient in a monstrous universe whose mechanism he can at best try to understand in part, without hope of controlling it. During the seventeenth century, on the contrary, man was profiting from discoveries made after the end of the Middle Ages and all through the marvels of the Renaissance, discoveries that were directly useful to him and delivered up the secrets of the world in which he lived. He became the clear-headed, self-appointed master of events; natural phenomena were now so comprehensible that it was possible to believe that he would one day dominate them entirely and bend them to his own uses.

The sixteenth century had presented man with the true dimensions of the world: the earth had become round and its limits were known. Science had brought to light fresh possibilities. The elation born of this new possession was not yet exhausted; it was to develop into an elegant, charming game during the eighteenth century before it gave rise to revolutionary passions. As for the seventeenth century, it was orderly even in the pursuit of pleasure. It could survey the past indulgently from the heights of its newly acquired certainties. Progress in science and politics corresponded with recent territorial discoveries. Original ideas in the realms of sociology and art corresponded with new concepts in philosophy and mathematics.

Everything was new. Byzantine, Roman and Gothic art were completely out of date, and belonged to primitive, unskilled times with elementary cultures; it was necessary to go much further back – to Greek or Roman antiquity – to find comparisons and examples to copy. In fact, the only living links with the past were religion and language; the language of learning and general culture, Latin, served to unite different countries, but disappeared from everyday life to give place to the national languages, which were also becoming stabilized and demonstrating their life and independence.

There were changes in the religious sphere as well. During the seventeenth century people ceased being satisfied with revealed religion; they wanted arguments, explanations and justifications. In every domain man naturally and aggressively took the lead as he had never done before. Palaces became more magnificent than churches, the clothes of noblemen and their wives more sumptuous than those of the saints.

This advance is reflected in taste; painting shows a preference for themes stressing man's importance, such as portraits, scenes of popular life or historical paintings. Even in religious painting one is definitely made aware of man's domination. All the figures are human; Christ and the saints may be wearing haloes but they are not differentiated from the other figures either in stature or character, as they were in Roman and Byzantine art. They are merely playing the principal part in a collective performance. Allegories are in favour: kings appear transformed into shining gods, seated on heavenly thrones and waited on by other divinities. Everything is dedicated to man and the glorification of his power.

Both noblemen and commoners had formerly adopted the flattering role of donor in order to get their portraits painted. They concealed their vanity beneath a humble demeanour and put themselves under the protection of their patron saints. But in the seventeenth century they abandoned patronage, and display became an end in itself; with inordinate vanity, they exhibited themselves exercising their functions and dressed in their finest clothes. Officers, magistrates and notabilities were surrounded by the attributes of their rank, or collected in self-important groups. A picture was a means of creating a permanent image of a temporary situation. Man thereby won a victory over the transience of his fate.

This state of affairs was obviously directly inspired by the Renaissance; one of its results was that the social function of artists was sensibly altered. They were in a hurry to be quit of the artisan status they had endured for so many centuries, and become privileged citizens who could make life gayer and grander for others. In the preceding century this role of decorating daily life had demanded exceptional qualities from the artists who fulfilled it, particularly in Italy. The more dazzlingly brilliant, those who left the deepest mark on their times, were always men of great culture, able to express themselves through different media. Da Vinci, Raphael, and Michelangelo are no exceptions; one could mention many others who, like them, were architects, painters, sculptors and engravers at one and the same time, in order to satisfy the demands of the rich patrons who employed them.

In France, when Francis I sent to Italy for men to build and decorate Fontainebleau, he followed the same principles in choosing Rosso, Niccolo dell' Abbate and Francesco Primaticcio. In the seventeenth century this still held good to some extent, but it tended to give way to specialization or a more definite individualism. The artist was becoming less and less of an artisan or even foreman, and insisted on each technique being independent of the rest. Specialization invited the creator to press his researches further into every department of his art, as well as facilitating self-expression, by no longer requiring of him complete submission to the general concept.

This differentiation between artist and artisan resulted from a conflict which went deeper than might appear at first sight and which had existed for a long time. The seventeenth century was the period when the issue finally came to a head. Painters, hitherto classed among artisans or manual workers, now wished their calling to be considered one of the 'noble arts', and were anxious to enjoy the corresponding privileges. At first they met with total opposition, on the plea that the noble arts (literature and music) spring directly and exclusively from the mind, without recourse to materials. However, it was at last agreed that painting and sculpture were not merely imitative techniques, and that the mind also played an important part in them. Theoretical discussions assumed ample proportions, especially in Italy, during the seventeenth century. This was the moment also when the new principles of perspective and the introduction of scientific ideas began to have a profound effect on the great painters, and to extend the domain of painting far beyond its religious functions.

Moreover, the discussions on art during the Council of Trent fostered the development of ideas and paved the way for the artist's new status. These ideas were to affect the hierarchy of the arts, for even among the 'noble arts' some are nobler than others, and each art has themes that are nobler than others. It became necessary therefore to establish a new order among the various genres.

In painting, the large composition (with a religious or historical subject) was ranked highest. Next came the portrait, then – infinitely less reputable – landscape, and finally still-life. In this way the various themes became independent, even if some took a lower rank. The Middle Ages had produced no painting devoted to landscape or still-life alone. From the beginning of the seventeenth century such specialization was not only allowed but became regular practice, so that in certain paintings the general composition was conceived by the master, while the execution of secondary figures, landscape and still-life was left to the hands of specialists in those genres. This manner of working shows the organization of a profession which was beginning to emphasize the artist's personality, in spite of some survivals of the artisan's anonymity, and which above all believed that intelligent rules could be framed for the almost automatic creation of beauty.

An age which aimed at control and rationality in everything did not hesitate to impose aesthetic principles on nature herself. Gardens 'in the French style', for instance, were the most astonishing evidence of this austerity; the designer would not allow the plants and trees to encroach on his preconceived plan, and the vegetation was confined to an extremely exact linear arrangement. Never had such complete obedience to man's laws been enacted, at any rate, in Italy.

This desire for power had certain advantages, but it also gave rise to a new risk of 'academicism', which never vanished. Wanting to make rules for everything, and believing that everything was subject to exact definition, led to over-systematization and a gradual diminution of the part played by self-expression. We are thus faced with a curious paradox: the century which was most concerned to emphasize the power of the individual was also responsible for framing principles to limit that power. And we see also the beginning of a permanent conflict, which was often epitomized in the opposition between the partisans of Rubens and Poussin, or between ancient and modern, but was, in fact, above all the clash between two artitudes towards works of art, each trend strengthened by the fact that it was the first time it had been allowed full play.

To gain a better understanding of this opposition and the various stages in the conflict, it may be useful to remember that what is called classical art embodies the desire for order, and requires the artist to conform to established rules and submit his inspiration to the control of reason. The classical painter organizes his composition according to principles that satisfy his intelligence; he is not content with unexpected effects. The opposing style, known as baroque, or rococo in the next century, and later on as romanticism, aims at an immediate impression, the effect of surprise and the attractiveness of liberty; it favours impulse, makes use of the unexpected, and tries to preserve something of the freshness of intuition in a work of art. The first is static, the second dynamic. It is clear that the opposition between these two currents must always have existed, but it had seemed less important during the preceding centuries and intervened relatively little in the production of works of art, since their purpose had been not self-expression for the artist but solely the satisfaction of the Church, which had commissioned them. After the

Renaissance, when works of art were no longer intended exclusively for the glorification of God but also to give pleasure to the men who created or ordered them, the artist's personality became more important, and the conflict (hitherto latent) between the different attitudes to works of art became one of the most interesting problems to both the public and the artist.

Each country played a different part, and some a very potent one, in this expansion of man's awareness through works of art, this affirmation of the individual. Italy, after several glorious centuries, appeared to be slowing up a little, as if she needed to get her breath back after all the contributions she had made. But she was to keep her brilliance for many lustra. Spain had taken her place among the greatest nations during the sixteenth century, through her conquests overseas and her alliance with central Europe, and was now in the most dazzling period of her history, before her decline. Flanders and the Low Countries were giving generous support to realistic and baroque art, while France had assimilated contributions from abroad to her own natural gifts to further the triumph of classicism.

Neither England, central Europe, nor Scandinavia witnessed the growth of any exceptional talents. Of course they echoed the ideas current in other countries, but at the same time traces of the Gothic period survived. England was preparing for the future by giving an exceedingly warm welcome to van Dyck, who abandoned his Flemish truculence to paint royal portraits and serve as prelude to the elegant portraitists of the eighteenth century. Germany produced nothing of permanent interest except the paintings of Elsheimer, who had not shaken free from the past. Poland showed particular sympathy towards the new ideas of baroque art; perhaps this should not be put down solely to the great attraction exercised by Italy, but also to a very definite desire to be connected with the culture of the West, rather than that of Russia, still deep in Byzantine influences.

Italy

It seems to us today that Italy occupied a secondary place in the roll of honour of the seventeenth century, and failed to produce the exceptional talents that came out of Spain, France and the Low Countries.

But this harsh judgment does not correspond to the facts as they appeared to those who lived at the time. For centuries past Italy had been enriching Western culture with a refinement, a sense of luxury and of the exquisite that had gradually liberated art from its religious functions. The influence of secular sources of inspiration even upon the most mystical works was beginning to be apparent, and there was some foundation for the anger of the reformers, who demanded more authority and a stricter control over works destined for the service of religion.

The Council of Trent came to an end in 1563, and its far-reaching consequences soon began to be felt. The Counter-Reformation was Italy's reply to the deliberate austerity of Protestantism. It offered the Church the pagan magnificence of the Renaissance, and the Church did not refuse to absorb the new trends. But she insisted on the strictest possible adherence to dogma and the most rigorous respect for Holy Writ in the production of holy images. In so doing she helped separate sacred and profane art, by emphasizing the development of the latter and adorning it with the charm of liberty.

Caravaggio (figs. 3–7)

Thanks to Raphael, da Vinci and Michelangelo, this wave of productiveness had spread far and wide. Caravaggio gave it more expressive power by the theatrical intensity of his realism and his completely new technique of introducing light as an active element in the composition of his pictures; his influence was to be considerable, and transform the vision of many painters of every nationality.

This was the situation at the end of the sixteenth century. If one is to go by dates of birth and death, Caravaggio belongs to the sixteenth century but, in fact, his influence lasted much longer, and from the beginning of the seventeenth century his light spread outside the limits of his own country. It was not so much that he invented a new technique, as that he offered a new attitude to painting. His dissociation from Christian art was not limited to his choice of themes; he introduced paganism into his attitude to his subject, even if it illustrated the life of a saint. Realism was made the pretext and excuse for embracing the truth more closely, being more faithful to life, and thereby making a more direct impression on the public. This notion of introducing brutally realistic ideas and giving them the greatest possible importance and expressive power was in itself a sign that he had departed from the attitude of the painters of the Middle Ages.

This pseudo-truthfulness, then, did not use the physical and material ingredients of the subject merely as adjuncts, but as active elements of the picture; for example, light no longer had a celestial and impersonal character as in primitive art. It played an emotional part; it modelled forms, accentuated contrasts and dramatized effects. Poses had lost the often rather gauche simplicity of those of holy personages; they belonged to living human beings, used to daily toil; muscles emphasized effort or fatigue, and stressed the physical situation of the moment, even in the case of the most sacred characters. The Venetians had already endowed colour and light with a suggestive power and independence derived from the living world. Caravaggio emphasized this character even more and thus originated a new notion of plastic lyricism, offering artists an infinite variety of possibilities. Of course, in so doing Caravaggio was effecting a revolution, but this was possible only because it corresponded to the expectations and tendencies of other artists: of the Venetians, for instance, as I have just said, and to some extent of Michelangelo or Leonardo da Vinci, who had also explored the possibilities of chiaroscuro before his day. But it was with Caravaggio that chiaroscuro became a system, and his name has been used to label and explain the spread of the movement known as Caravaggism throughout Europe.

A few years saw the disappearance of the last great Italian masters: Titian died in 1576, Veronese in 1588, Tintoretto in 1594, Annibale Carracci in 1609, and Caravaggio in 1610. They left behind them a great reputation which cast a glow over their successors and made Italy an irresistible centre of attraction for artists of all nationalities. Italian painters continued to be faithful to these ideas and principles, but they were shorter of breath than the pioneers had been. They transformed those ideas and principles into formulae and, though they had enough skill to preserve the illusion for a while and retain a reputation among their contemporaries, it was none the less evident that the future was not in their hands. Italy had set a multiple example; she had opened roads leading in the most varied directions and revealed original resources available to thought and imagination. She had started Europe on a course which was destined to give Western culture its individual character. She left the task of developing these resources and innovations to others. But she still enjoyed such prestige and held so many secrets in her power that she was to continue for many lustra teaching her lesson to the innumerable foreigners who came to her for enlightenment. Her best painters founded schools and transmitted to their pupils the necessary formulae for the creation of masterpieces.

The Carracci

The Carracci family was to play an important part in extending the light shed by the works of the great masters to the period after their death. The two brothers Annibale (figs. 1 and 2) and Agostino and their cousin Ludovico, all three passionately devoted to the cause of painting, travelled, and set themselves to analyse the techniques of Veronese, Titian and Correggio; besides producing their own works, they were eager to communicate what they had learnt. In 1585 they founded a school in Bologna, which was under the direction of Ludovico until his death in 1619 and had a considerable influence. In it they taught the exact science of carefully drawn and defined form, which led to a new phase of mannerism, because this systematic instruction gave the pupils the means and illusion of science without plumbing the depths of the subject, or perhaps leaving enough room for a strong individuality to develop along its own lines.

Guido Reni (fig. 11), Guercino (fig. 18), and Domenichino (fig. 10)
At this time, at least in Italy, the art of painting was pursued with passion, with such passion as to cause surprisingly violent behaviour. It was carried on in a stormy and often unbridled atmosphere, amid relentless jealousy and rivalry which did not shrink from criminal acts. Each painter believed that he possessed a particular vision in conflict with that of the others; excess manifested itself in the most diverse ways. Several artists from the Carracci's school at Bologna had a considerable success. There was such enthusiasm for the work of Guido Reni that some thought him greater than Raphael, and Caravaggio considered having him assassinated. Guercino's reputation was so great that Count Aldobrandini installed him in a luxurious palace in Bologna, where the highest in the land were proud to visit him. Domenichino was Carracci's collaborator as well as his pupil, and he can be considered the last representative of the group. In fact, all this agitation was centred round the ideas formulated by Caravaggio, and tended either towards academicism or to the introduction of a lyrical realism which was to serve the future development of what is called baroque art.

In this new development, Bernini's name must be coupled with Caravaggio's; his influence was at least as strong, in that he complemented Caravaggio's work as a painter by bringing a similar richness to sculpture and architecture. With this baroque style – sometimes also called the Jesuit style – which triumphed in Rome during the seventeenth century, he endowed architecture with new forms of decoration, embellishments, arabesques and unexpected convolutions, and originated a current which we find thereafter throughout Western art. In Caravaggio's paintings and Bernini's sculpture the figures have been made somewhat theatrical in order to express violent emotions; the Virgins seem to be swooning, lit up by a refined sensuality. Men and gods have projecting muscles, and are enveloped in shining, floating stuffs, puffed out with wind. Even when they express austerity, gestures are emphatic. This state of mind found its most finished expression in Bernini's sculpture and its apotheosis in certain parts of the decoration of St Peter's at Rome. The marble has taken on a silky, watered suppleness. Bernini and Caravaggio are two aspects of a single need, of a single emotion, and it is unthinkable to treat them separately. To such a point that, even when it is only painting that is under consideration, the name of Bernini cannot be omitted from any description of this very original phase in the history of art.

Spain

After conquering vast territories abroad, after being on the point of consolidating her unity in Europe with an immense empire under Charles V in the preceding century, Spain put the coping-stone on the edifice of her power by finally driving out the Moors at the beginning of the seventeenth century. This century was, however, to see the beginning of her decadence, though she was not yet aware of it any more than Italy had been. Like Italy, she embarked on her own decline in triumphal style but, with her prosperity and power at their summit, she had not yet exhausted her creative powers even after her first great defeats. She had not worked out her basic principles nor fulfilled all her possibilities; her peculiar originality had not yet been personified in men of genius and modes of expression capable of summing up and illustrating it. That was to be the role of the seventeenth century. In the sixteenth century the genius of El Greco had been one of those manifestations through which a nation recognizes and discovers itself. However, this miraculous flower did not exhaust the strength of the plant. Spain was radiating power, confident in her own strength and vitality. She fostered the growth of remarkable painters, whose profoundly original contributions remained more or less on the margin of the rest of European art. Elsewhere the Renaissance had inspired a longing for happiness, for an easy life, a pagan desire for enjoyment, and an appetite for gaiety and luxury. In Spain, austerity was still the distinguishing mark of power. The desire for greatness was stronger than the desire for pleasure; there was more constraint than liberty in the physical conditions of life. In the Low Countries, France and Italy, the extension of ideas about art and its relation to society caused an improvement in living conditions and in the level of culture for a great many citizens, and created a favourable climate for the development of outstanding personalities; in Spain we see a more explosive impulse and a group of masters so exceptionally talented that one thinks of their individual qualities rather than what unites them with their epoch. One might speculate as to whether they were the emanation of their epoch or whether, on the contrary, it was created by them. Their dimensions are such that they seem over life-size.

In literature such men as Cervantes (died in 1616) and Lope de Vega (died in 1635) are symbolic of this exceptional creative force. Of course, they belong in part to the sixteenth century, but they do much to give the seventeenth its special emphasis. Essentially Spanish as they are, they go beyond national boundaries and are of universal significance. As for the painters, they strike us even more than the writers of the seventeenth century as isolated individuals, but they left such an intensely personal imprint on their times that it does not occur to one to ask whether their greatness is in harmony with the preoccupations of most of their contemporaries.

The 'Golden Century', as it has been called, can be summed up in a few names. Velázquez, Ribera, Zurbarán and Murillo had no need to be surrounded by devotees and followers or affiliated to a group, as happened elsewhere, for their inspiration and the development of their gifts to be understood. They shone dazzlingly enough to reach the highest summits of art.

The royal collections of this period are magnificent and contain many masterpieces by Titian, Tintoretto and Rubens. They prove that culture reached a very high level at the beginning of the century. But the greatest Spanish painters did not really owe much to the brilliance of Italy (even though most of them went there) except perhaps a certain sympathy with Caravaggism and its dramatic use of light to make reality more intensely alive, and so impose an exaggerated style upon it. To be more exact, they had assimilated Italian painting so completely that one has the impression of an entirely original creative impulse, just as in the preceding century El Greco had produced typically Spanish painting derived from Tintoretto.

Realism

Realism flourished in Spain more than elsewhere, but it was used not so much in the cause of physical truth as in order to give the subject more emotional intensity. This realism is to be seen not only in Ribera's romantic monsters, Váldes Leal's macabre inventions and Murillo's tender Virgins surrounded by smiling cherubs (fig. 37), but also in the frozen elegance of Zurbarán's saints (fig. 44) or the austerely tense faces of his Franciscan monks.

This realism was pushed so far that it is possible to see in it the beginning of the cult of ugliness which was to continue under various guises during the following centuries and has been an active ferment in our own. The beauty of ugliness was first upheld in Spain during this period. Of course, other painters of other days and other countries had already been inspired by monsters. Those of Hieronymus Bosch or Brueghel, for instance, are products of whimsicality, an ironical imagination, or caricature, and do not touch deeply upon life itself or deny the existence of ideal beauty; but Ribera's cripples exalt with almost passionate zeal all that is physically and humanly most aggressive in ugliness, in bodies destroyed by illness and misery. Whereas in every other country one is aware of a desire for moderation even in the most tempestuous outbursts, in Spain one finds a restless craving for excess. When this ardour is restrained the result is perhaps even more disturbing, as in Velázquez's dwarfs (figs. 31 and 33), or even the set faces of some of his infantas.

The Influence of Religion

To understand the tension visible in Spanish painting, we must also take into account the special development of religious emotion in Spain, shown by the fact that the Inquisition was much harsher there than elsewhere. Religious orders multiplied and became all-powerful. They were among the most important patrons of art. They commissioned great series of frescoes representing the life of a saint or an order, each series covering the walls of an entire room.

In Spain religious subjects prevailed even when non-religious painting of every description was rapidly spreading elsewhere; she had practically speaking no landscape-painters. Apart from a few rare exceptions, Velázquez in particular, there were no nudes. Perhaps, as some writers have suggested, this was because of the threefold influence of the Catholics, the Moors and the Jews.

Even in portraiture, religious pressure is seen in the 'portraits in the divine manner', which represented the sitter with saintly attributes. This is found in several of Zurbarán's works and gives the paintings a somewhat irreligious elegance, which might seem overdone if they adhered strictly to the subject. In the same way there are very few compositions with mythological subjects, except for one or two by Ribera and Velázquez, and these seem as if the painter had taken the chance to paint realistically, once liberated from the restrictions imposed on religious subjects.

Still-Life

One of the results of this access of realism was the development of still-life, or *bodegon* as it was called. Here one sees Caravaggism in its most interesting form, with its peculiar manner of bathing the object in light and making the forms live, not only by means of definite outline, but also by frankly affirming shadows and contours. This treatment of the object is typical of Velázquez's domestic scenes as well as his still-lifes. The figures are observed with the same implacable severity as the still-life objects. It is also characteristic of Zurbarán, though in him the influences of Caravaggism is indirect; his style is none the less lucid, and gives off a strangely potent and suggestive poetry.

But if one can see Caravaggism both in Velázquez and Zurbarán, their techniques are entirely different, almost opposed. Just as Zurbarán's forms are firmly and exactly circumscribed by a living line, in Velázquez the transition from one volume to another or one plane to another is achieved by infinitely skilful and subtle gradations which bind together all the details of the composition. Even in their brushwork they are opposed; Zurbarán's paint is smooth and polished, while Velázquez uses separate touches to create a changing atmosphere, with a technique that the Impressionists were to adopt later on.

Still-life, in Spain even more than in other countries, became a form of plastic organization which left the painter freer than any other subject. He could arrange its elements as he liked, creating very deliberate harmonies of form and colour, characterized by a certain aridity, but rich with concentrated thought. This approach to still-life had certain similarities with that adopted, several centuries later, by the Cubists, and one is often tempted to compare Zurbarán and Juan Gris.

With Sánchez Cotán, who belongs to the generation before that of the artists just mentioned, we are already among orderly still-lifes, composed almost like abstracts, but with a mystery and secret suggestiveness emanating from scrupulously reproduced realism, re-echoed in our time by the seductive and disturbing works of the Surrealists.

'Vanities'

A similar disturbing quality in more brutal form is found in the numerous 'vanities' of the period. These summonses to meditation, with their easy symbolism, juxtaposing a candle, a book, an hour-glass and a skull, were often puerile affairs, but in Spanish hands they had a haunting grandeur, especially in those of Váldes Leal.

Portraits

This affirmation, or perhaps affectation of austerity, did not however exclude a taste for ostentation, which is apparent in most of the portraits; their beautiful clothes trimmed with gold, and their heavy jewelry give some idea of the pomp with which the nobility liked to surround themselves, and of the fabulous fortunes founded on the conquests of the previous century. There were no collective portraits in Spain, as in Flanders. Spanish exhibitionism was prouder, less childish and less easily satisfied. Each man wanted to stand alone rather than be measured by comparison with others.

The Spaniards added their own peculiar harshness and austerity to the taste for ostentation and richness of the Renaissance, the rather mannered refinement of Italian culture, and the overt lyricism of the Flemish, without abandoning that dramatic grandeur which left its impress on simple and familiar poses. The result corresponded to the superficial mannerism of Italian painting, but struck an infinitely more serious note of pathos.

Zurbarán (figs. 39–45)

Zurbarán is the painter who gave most intense expression to the magic and silence, the generosity and severity, the austerity and violence of Spanish painting. He is a particularly good example, perhaps because, as one of the few great painters of the age who never went to Italy, he shows the extent of Italian influence, the strength of Spanish opposition to it, and the limits to its acceptance.

Zurbarán, more than anyone else of his time, was able to express the intensity of religious emotion by his powerful concentration on every detail, even those of his still-lifes (fig. 43). It is interesting to see how well he succeeded in preserving the impression of the isolation of each object in a still-life, and the silent poetry of the Gothic painters, while applying the light and shadow values of Caravaggism. Like Caravaggio he insisted on his faces expressing intense feeling, whether in scenes with figures, or in portraits. But whereas in Caravaggio this led to a more or less affected concentration on outward appearances, with Zurbarán one always has the impression of a mask reflecting the thoughts within.

Velázquez (figs. 28–35)

Zurbarán was a friend of Velázquez, and the latter's work can from many points of view be seen as belonging essentially to the same period and with affinities in common, but his method of composition, his structural technique and the sentiments it expresses are very different. In fact, the austerity which indicates a mystical concentration in Zurbarán, is in Velázquez above all a sign of attention to the methods and resources of his art. Velázquez's work has the greater right to be called 'pure painting'. One feels that he is essentially, perhaps solely, concerned with problems of painting, and his art may be considered as one of the highest achievements of painting of all time.

Whether he paints peasants or noblemen, clowns or infantas, Velázquez is never the slave of his subject, even in his historical pictures; he arranges his composition; he applies his colours to give the required values; he places his figures or objects so as to create the space he has planned. There is an air of certainty in his perfection; he is confident of being a master of technique, and everything else – whether of sentimental or literary interest – is merely an adjunct.

The conflict between the opposing principles of baroque and classical art, which was to arise during the seventeenth century, does not apply to him. He was baroque in so far as he used certain discoveries of Caravaggism, such as chiaroscuro, but he would have nothing to do with affected poses. He was classical in that his sense of moderation made him shun excess and always aim at a certain order in his work and exactness in his design. But, in spite of this, he cannot be accused of dryness. Some of his portraits of infantas, for instance, seem to have very definite outlines but, by studying them more closely and investigating their technique, one discovers that the limits between the different forms are suggested by skilful transitions from one tone to another, so much so that even his most pronounced contrasts are never violent. His most famous composition, *Las Meninas* in the Prado, gives one the impression of being both neutral in tone and richly coloured at the same time.

His great mastery of his art allowed him to undertake the most diverse subjects with equal success; he approached domestic interiors as seriously as historical scenes, portraits of peasants with as much respect as those of great noblemen, and a simple still-life with as much exactness and care as a composition on a grand scale.

Ribera (figs. 24–7)

At the opposite extreme to Velázquez and Zurbarán is Ribera, a powerful incarnation of Spanish Caravaggism. Ribera adopted Caravaggio's exaggerated, even excessive realism, but he exalted the dramatic element instead of the vitality. The Spanish taste for monstrosities was gratified in his horrifying beggars and cripples; their twisted limbs, ravaged faces and tattered clothes are not presented as picturesque, but with a sort of dramatic nobility, and they reveal an indifference to the rest of the world which emerges as pride in not concealing their wretchedness. The most declamatory romantic painting, two centuries later, was not more forceful than Ribera's; the violent contrasts between light and shadow are a prelude to the exalted mood of the nineteenth century, though they avoid its affectation.

Murillo (figs. 36–8)

The most remarkable feature of Spanish seventeenth-century painting is that it carried every genre as far as possible even, one might say, with excessive brutality, without ever being affected or seeming artificial. Even Murillo's more pleasing art, whose attractions seem to us a little insipid today, never relapses into preciosity. His earnest sweetness prepares the way for the simpering style of some eighteenth-century painters, yet Murillo is an example of the effect of Flemish influences. (Flanders remained under Spanish rule until 1700.) There were, in fact, frequent interchanges between the two countries. Rubens had gone twice to Spain as ambassador, and many of his paintings were in royal collections or those of connoisseurs; besides which, Flemish artists had been delighted to go to Spain and Spanish artists to Flanders, for long periods at a time. Engravings had also helped to spread knowledge of Flemish and Italian painting.

These circumstances must be borne in mind if we wish to understand the position held by Murillo and the reasons for his success. All that he had to contribute – the foretaste of eighteenth-century sentimentality, his refinement, the tender quality of his faith – seemed new in a country where greater harshness was the rule. This new departure did not seem banal as it does to us at the present time, when we are certainly unfair to Murillo in failing to give his skill and charm the appreciation they deserve.

Velázquez, on the contrary, stands in the impregnable position of a great master; his perfection sets him beyond criticism. He is not in yesterday's fashion nor yet today's. He had no political axe to grind: noblemen and humble peasants alike found an impartial and attentive observer in him. He does not even give support to any aesthetic theory: devotees of realism and supporters of classicism find him equally satisfying. With an audacity that has the appearance of simplicity he is solely and entirely a painter.

Pacheco, de Herrera the Elder (fig. 23), Ribalta, Coello and Mayno (fig. 22)
The other Spanish painters revolved round these great names, preceding or following them without adding anything very new; nor is it surprising that they had less influence in other countries. However, several of them had considerable and deserved success within their limits. And they make the great masters seem less isolated.

Pacheco was a master whose lessons influenced many, particularly his son-in-law Velázquez. We are indebted to him for a number of portraits and the publication of *The Art of Painting*, a summary of many of the ideas of the period. De Herrera the Elder began as a mannerist and moved on to realism; he had affinities with Zurbarán, who finished the series of paintings started by him in the church of San Buenaventura at Seville.

Francisco Ribalta was closer to El Greco and was Ribera's master. Claudio Coello can be considered the most important painter of the Madrid School at the end of the seventeenth century, and was a remarkable decorator with unusual skill in composing scenes with long perspectives. Mayno has sometimes been compared with justification to the French painter Georges de la Tour, which gives a clear idea of his brand of Caravaggism.

There were others too who bore witness to Spain's active and widespread participation in a movement which was really the affirmation of man's superiority and pride in his liberation.

Flanders

Flemish painting of the seventeenth century developed in an atmosphere and social climate somewhat like that of the Venetian School in the preceding century. Prosperity came from the same source in both, affected the same classes of society and had the same results on the evolution of taste: busy towns, enriched by trade, were controlled by powerful municipal bodies representing a population of ship-owners and enterprising merchants; exporters made quick fortunes and kept in contact with the outside world, hearing of Oriental splendours from the enthusiastic and often exaggerated accounts of travellers. Material success led to display; even in private life prodigality and a taste for luxury soon made their appearance; social advancement brought with it a love of ostentation. While the French court was gradually building art on foundations that had been developing since the beginning of the Renaissance, the suddenly prosperous citizens of Flanders were offered more accessible art that was less linked to the past.

Rubens (figs. 63–70)

Rubens was for the north what Titian and Tintoretto were for the Mediterranean. He abounded with creative impulses which only asked room to unfold. He acted more than once as special ambassador on successful political missions to Italy, Spain, France and England. Many of his intimate friends were men of the highest culture. His travels made him well-informed, his work shows that his mind was open to new influences and his art collection reveals what an attraction antiquity had for him, so that, after his first visit to Italy and his contact with the splendours of Venice, Rubens became a perfect product of the Renaissance. He gave an irresistible new impulse to Flemish art just at the moment when it was being swayed by opposing currents and its future seemed uncertain. And there were political and religious causes also behind both the differences and uniformity to be found in Flemish art of the period.

During the preceding centuries there had been little reason to distinguish Flemish art proper from that of the rest of the Netherlands, but the seventeenth century, by separating the political destinies of the provinces, had a profound effect on their spiritual evolution. The north, by freeing itself from Spanish dominion, was able to shake off Catholicism and take over the new Protestant discipline; while the south, on the contrary, was still under Spain and remained one of the last strongholds of Catholicism in northern Europe, which had now almost entirely freed itself from Rome. Baroque art was almost more political than aesthetic in origin. It found one of its most potent forms of expression in Rubens's work and, through him, reached an international audience unrivalled by any other country.

The end of the sixteenth century had witnessed the Duke of Alba's terrible dictatorship, and it seemed as if the southern provinces might be left for a long while in an impoverished condition, incapable of regaining any of the brilliance they had known under the Renaissance. But Rubens's genius found these very circumstances propitious, and soon inspired art with new energy, fed by the renewed eagerness for life. For the destruction of the iconoclasts he substituted production on so generous a scale that a single man's life was not enough: he ran his studio like a business enterprise, with a great many collaborators and specialists in every subject.

There was no duplicity about this sharing out of tasks; everyone knew of it and it surprised no one. Rubens had a scale of prices, to be agreed on with the client when a work was commissioned. The highest price was charged for a work entirely painted by the master, a lower one when he only carried out part of it and was helped by his most brilliant assistants, and the lowest price of all meant that it had been left to his pupils to carry out from his sketches, and that Rubens himself only made a few necessary corrections to the picture at the end. Rubens had travelled a great deal before he became a master of his art and organization; he had profited from the rich art of Spain, and even more from that of Italy. His genius was great enough to accept the lessons these countries had to teach, and make use of them in his own way. It is obvious that Venetian painting – the passion expressed in Tintoretto's tortured bodies and the intensity of Titian's compositions – had deeply impressed the Flemish artist. It was these impressions that nourished his lyrical sensuality and were the cause of his complete breach with earlier Flemish art, the simple placid realism of the Primitives, or Brueghel's picturesque detail and careful, sometimes grotesque observation. However, Rubens owed his deep feeling for humanity and daily life to his Flemish temperament. Even in his mythological pictures, his gods are always basically human (fig. 66); even in his religious pictures, holiness remains linked to physical sensation – the pain or joy on the faces of his figures belong to this earth (figs. 65 and 67–70).

In this way, while adhering to the principles of baroque, Rubens introduced into the religious art of his day a pagan element which had never been equalled, or so confidently and naturally displayed, even by Caravaggio. There were so many new possibilities in his work that its influence radiated far beyond geographical frontiers. Rubens's paganism makes that of the Italian Renaissance seem very temperate, and well under the control of classical principles. This is because, instead of moderation and tradition, Rubens brought to his work an exuberant sensuality, already foreshadowed in Brueghel's coarseness. But while Brueghel found his inspiration in popular and peasant life, Rubens's sumptuous art was acceptable to the courts of Europe, and indeed sought after by them.

His paganism emerged not only in the appearance and poses of his figures, but also in the settings of his still-lifes and landscapes – in the material aspects of life, in fact. I have already said that it was during the seventeenth century that landscape and still-life came into their own in all countries, so that it is useless to claim this change in the choice of themes as due to Rubens's influence alone. All the same, these subjects undoubtedly expanded in his hands, and he has left canvases which will always be mentioned as fine examples of them.

We must not forget the part played by his collaborators. Rubens knew how to make the best use of them. By modifying the proportion between the various elements in a composition, he invented a new way of understanding nature and giving her a more active role. And the more insistent he was on introducing elements which had hitherto been subsidiary, such as landscape and still-life, the more often Rubens had to rely on specialists in these genres to help him in his work. It is usual to distinguish two sorts of helpers: firstly his pupils, and secondly his more independent collaborators, with reputations of their own, who consented to work with him.

Rubens's Studio

Rubens's studio, taken as a whole, was the most active centre of Flemish painting in the seventeenth century. This has naturally led to an excess of attributions, and the number of paintings nowadays ascribed to the master is so great that one wonders whether a good many of them may not be by other hands. This is possible, or even probable, but it does not affect the aesthetic problem, or the general atmosphere of the epoch. Not long ago, for instance, an art historian tried to prove that a great many pictures attributed to Rubens were really by Snyders (fig. 79), who is usually thought of as a still-life painter. He certainly worked in Rubens's studio as a specialist in this genre, but it is also known that he carried out some large compositions of his own which appear to have been lost.

It is surely evidence of Rubens's great influence that he had among his collaborators some admirable painters, who would have been the glory of their country on their own account, painters such as Jordaens (figs. 55 and 56) and van Dyck (figs. 71–3) for instance. Nor did the work they did for him prevent their own painting from being on a high creative level. Jordaens's drinking scenes are sometimes even coarser and more exuberant than those of Rubens; but they are also more disciplined. Van Dyck, for his part, escaped from this over-strong influence as soon as he could. Once in England, he became so much part of the country that he may be considered as one of the greatest English portrait-painters, perhaps even as one of the creators of English art, in the same way that El Greco was of Spanish art, although he was born a Greek and brought up in Italy. Van Dyck avoided Rubens's rather vulgar coarseness, and developed an extremely elegant style, where we find richer colours harmonizing with a range of more austere greys and blacks, and a free and lively draughtsmanship instead of mere virtuosity.

Another of Rubens's collaborators was Jan Brueghel (figs. 57–62), son of the great Brueghel, who specialized in painting landscapes, animals and floral accessories.

But even when they had not actually worked with Rubens, most

Flemish painters of the day owed him something, or followed in his wake. Momper was one of the best landscape-painters, already showing a hint of eighteenth-century romanticism; he avoided the plunging perspectives typical of the sixteenth century and had a more realistic, though often monochrome, conception of landscape. Jan Fyt (fig. 53) belonged, like Snyders, to the series of painters who introduced heaped-up pyramids of food into their still-lifes, giving a new richness to this hitherto pedestrian subject. Caspar de Crayer (fig. 52) came under Rubens's influence but never developed enough spirit to be his rival. His work is to all intents and purposes an imitation, but infinitely more superficial.

Among the portraitists descended from Rubens, the Pourbus family must be mentioned, especially Frans Pourbus the Younger, who was faithful to his father's memory and so to the aesthetic of the sixteenth century, but yet reacted to the influences of his day. He therefore bridges over the two centuries and proves that there was no definite breach between their traditions. In my section on French painting I will discuss the portraits he painted in that country. Cornelis de Vos, who worked in Rubens's studio, must also be mentioned among portraitists; while his brother Paul de Vos specialized in animal paintings and hunting scenes (fig. 54).

Finally, we ought to include the name of David Teniers among the Flemish-born painters. He studied under his father and, although he was influenced by Rubens, he developed a style of anecdotal genre (figs. 74–6) that brings him closer in spirit to contemporary Dutch painters. Teniers spent most of his life at Antwerp, but from 1651 to 1656 he was in Brussels, working as court painter and taking care of Archduke Leopold Wilhelm's important collection of pictures.

The Netherlands

In the panorama of seventeenth-century European painting the Netherlands was the country which most completely summed up the art of the time, most clearly indicated how it developed from the past and whither it was tending in the future, and provided the greatest number of gifted artists, including men of genius and of varied temperaments.

When confronted by human genius one is inclined to wonder what chance or combination of favourable circumstances has caused this special concentration of spiritual qualities in the person, place and time in question. We see other countries achieving their independence and individual character under the dominating influence of one or two artists of genius: Velázquez in Spain, Rubens in Flanders, Poussin in France, and Caravaggio in Italy. Each of these is so conspicuously pre-eminent that the art of his day seems to be organized around him, and all other painters, whether in sympathy or opposition to him, fall into the second rank, even if they actually have more success. In Holland it is impossible to impose such a rigorous hierarchy centred round one man; the greatest among them does not exclude the claims of the rest, and more than one deserves to be put in the first rank. Though Rembrandt's name is the first to enter one's mind, though his work is on such a gigantic scale that it sometimes seems almost fabulous, it does not exhaust the possibilities. In a quite different domain Vermeer is also a unique phenomenon, undimmed by Rembrandt's glory. And even Frans Hals expresses such intense and exceptional humanity that he stands apart from Rembrandt, although resemblances can be found between the two artists, rather in their choice of themes than in their technique or inspiration.

In Holland, then, we see an amazing florescence, in which the new functions and aims of art and the new links between the artist and his public were more completely and clearly epitomized than elsewhere. No doubt this was partly due to the fact that, by adopting Protestantism and liberating itself from the Church of Rome, Holland had begun to take a more ambitious view of individual liberty and man's responsibilities to himself. With Protestantism, the politics, art and private life of the Netherlands, as well as its way of thinking, took a fresh direction. For one thing Protestant chapels had to conform to severe new regulations which forbade any decoration, especially holy figures or images. Religious painting virtually ceased. At a time when it was expanding and being enriched in other countries by the obviously pagan influence of baroque, it was unacceptable in Holland for, even though Rembrandt still maintained his right to take themes from the Scriptures, it was the human not the sacred significance of the subjects and personages that interested him.

It is of course possible to see Rembrandt as one of the offshoots of Caravaggism, since he too insisted on light and contrast playing a psychological part in his pictures, or even being the chief actors in the drama. But his purpose and his inspiration were the opposite of those of Italian art; in his mature work we find silence instead of declamation, and concentration instead of gesticulation – though this does not prevent his work from burning with a steadier glow than the lyrical outbursts of Italy.

In Holland, even more than in Flanders, the painter's public was made up of merchants and ship-owners. The wealthy were all-powerful but showed no desire for expansion. Their dealings with countries overseas did not trouble the heads of these burgesses; their new religion kept their minds within more familiar every-day and austere limits. They seemed to be aware that a new society was growing around them and that victory consisted in practical accomplishment rather than territorial conquest. Man was becoming a man, neither more nor less. Italian daydreams, Rubens's sumptuous effects, French grandeur roused no access of enthusiasm in citizens who knew how to reckon their resources and capacities They had comfortable houses, and handsome, solid furniture; the setting in which they lived was harmonious. Their pictures were in the same key.

Since there was no occasion for energy and enthusiasm to be vented on wild enterprises and exaggerated representations of them, humbler subjects became the fashion and were to be seen in the best pictures. There are many examples of Dutch seventeenth-century art proving that the intensity of a painting is not in the subject but in the painter's inner emotional life. In the greatest masterpieces of the age – and they rank among the masterpieces of Western painting of all time – the subjects are unimportant: Rembrandt's *The Jewish Bride* or *The Syndics*, Vermeer's *View of Delft*, Frans Hals's *The Women Governors of the Haarlem Almshouse* are among the highest achievements of art and arouse the utmost admiration, yet what they represent is absolutely without interest. The only thing that counts in a picture is the painting – that is the extremely modern lesson we were taught three centuries ago by a nation of merchants, newly awakened to their responsibilities as men, and in process of becoming a society of scholars, philosophers and painters, devoted to the new spiritual values.

The first result, as I have said, was the disappearance of religious painting. A parallel development was that themes hitherto despised, such as genre painting, landscape and still-life, advanced in the general esteem. Something of the same sort was happening in other countries, proving that the current was a general one, and that Western thought was at that moment detaching itself, in part at least, from sacred subjects and turning to the external world. Man was watching himself live, and observing his surroundings. But in no other country was this more clearly and completely visible than in Holland.

Landscape Painting

Landscape was probably the first new theme to come into its own. Avercamp (fig. 102), with his skating scenes on frozen rivers, was in the tradition of the previous century – the century so marvellously illustrated by Brueghel, whose works make one wonder whether he used landscape as a pretext for scenes of picturesque life, or if, on the contrary, the amusing fantasy animating his figures was a pretext for interpreting a landscape, its atmosphere, light, the density and freshness of the air. With Ruysdael (figs. 100 and 101) no misunderstanding is possible. The artist has penetrated the naturel world, entered into its life, become one with its vegetation, and been inspired to linger in front of a ray of sunlight, a tree or a copse. There is no paganism about his communing with nature, only an intimately personal poetic feeling, without artifice or need to create fables, divine or otherwise.

Holland refused to take the Church as intermediary, preferring to hold direct converse with God; she would have nothing to do with alien mythologies, even light-heartedly. And just as in her faith she wanted direct contact with God, in her life she wanted direct contact with things. Her art is the affirmation of the individual, whether he is observer or observed. Each tree in Ruysdael's and Hobbema's (figs. 112 and 113) landscapes is 'that tree' and no other. It is not a symbolic tree or an abstract sign, it is a portrait. We find something of the same sharp individuality in nineteenth-century painting of the Barbizon School, and this compels me to say again that the seventeenth century is as it were a preface to the nineteenth, since interest in reality leads to the discovery of the poetic resources of nature. While other countries were still producing idealized landscapes, in Holland we find them representing reality, even if that reality was a reflection of their creator.

The Dutch countryside with its remote horizons is structurally different from that of other countries. It does not summon up a series of ascending parallel planes such as we find in French or Italian classicism, but presents us with an immense sky, descending low over the land. The vertical line made by a tree or a steeple takes on a special significance, like a signal in space. The artist must renounce vast panoramas, with views plunging into the distance. His feet are on the ground, at the level of daily life, and he gazes attentively at the brightness around him. In Dutch landscapes and in those of no other country, one feels that the world consists of three harmonious elements: earth, water and sky. Everything leads back to this trinity and the light that bathes it. The sky itself is a living space, with colour, rhythm, dimensions and substance.

Ruysdael and Hobbema make us pause in this humid countryside and its vegetation that is romantic before its time. Van Goyen (figs. 93 and 94), van de Velde (fig. 121) and van der Heyden (fig. 131) generally preferred boating scenes whose animation foreshadows the eighteenth rather than the nineteenth century. Paulus Potter (fig. 97) and Albert Cuyp (fig. 120) underlined the everyday aspect of places by means of their interest in animals – horses and cows. Momper's view of life was more agitated.

Whether they are empty or enlivened by a crowd of figures, the important, the essential thing in all these landscapes is nature – man's new intimacy with his surroundings. In the previous centuries the Gothic painters had observed, analysed and described, making careful and detailed inventories of the external world. Each tree and object had an independent, almost solitary existence, even in large compositions with figures. In the seventeenth century it was not so much a question of taking possession of nature, as of coming to terms with a complex whole and participating in a life made up of a number of combined elements. Sometimes this was carried even further: physical sensation was reinforced by an emotional content which might be so strong that it seemed to be the true subject of the picture. In the hands of the best painters of the period a landscape could be identified with a state of mind. Some of Rembrandt's landscapes, for instance, give off an almost oppressive intensity of emotion; and there is an obsessional quality in the implacable calm, intense stillness and subtle light of Vermeer's *View of Delft*. The poetry and silence of this picture will never be surpassed, nor the subject be more completely dominated by a feeling of inwardness.

Street Scenes

I have shown that man's intimacy with the external world gave rise to a new conception of landscape, whether of town or country. Urban subjects, however, necessitated different modes of expression, almost a new vocabulary. Here we see quiet alleys, lined with neat rows of brick houses, given a regular rhythm by their doors and windows: it is an almost purely geometric form of art, made up of straight lines, and apparently as different as possible from the landscapes of the countryside. The silence and immobility of these street scenes distil poetry, and the passing moment is transfixed. In this department Vermeer once again showed himself a master capable of transforming reality. Pieter de Hoogh was interested in the same themes and showed the same qualities but in a lesser degree; his poetry is essentially similar but without the indefinable sense of the miraculous which marks out Vermeer as a genius.

Interiors

The logical consequence of the interest which the painters of this century showed in daily life, landscape and town scenes was that they pursued their researches indoors, and scenes of domestic life appeared in abundance. The Gothic painters had chosen religious subjects, and given their annunciations or nativities Dutch or Flemish settings. This was no longer necessary; secular life had acquired the freedom of the cities. Man stood face to face with himself, without ally or protector, before a mirror as faithful as a camera.

Here again light played an important part. In landscape it was often evenly spread over the canvas in a vibrant film, impartially illuminating every detail in an indefinite, aerial space. In interiors, on the contrary, its shape and limits were clearly defined, and it penetrated horizontally through side windows, dividing the picture-space regularly into successive planes clearly accentuated by regions of shadow, and emphasizing the geometrical character that we noticed in the street scenes. In the foremost rank of such painters we shall again find the names of Vermeer (figs. 114, 116, 117 and 119) and Pieter de Hoogh (figs. 129 and 130). Women at ease or at work inhabit these middle-class dwellings where life unrolls smoothly and without ostentation, where comfort is valued above luxury, where the furniture is solid and simple and every object is pleasing. Order and meticulous cleanliness is the rule, and there is no room for passion.

Yet this atmosphere does not give an impression of indifference. On the contrary, one is aware of a subtle presence, a silent respect for life, a sort of attentive, patient earnestness, which is even more apparent in the church interiors. Saenredam (fig. 96), among others, applied his delicate skill and gentle observation to this genre, translating a religious emotion devoid of violence into terms of pale grey tones.

Everywhere we find this honest realism: in the life of the fields or of the town, the orderliness of houses or of consciences, in scenes of noisy gaiety as well as of peaceful good behaviour. A great many minor masters contributed to this form of art, and faithfully represented the moderation in deed and thought of patrons who found their satisfaction in home life and had none of the desire for excess shown in other countries.

These minor masters have not of course the purity of Vermeer or Pieter de Hoogh; their art is less exact. Often irony or a taste for the fantastic attracted them to the more picturesque aspects of daily life, to less innocent occupations than music or household duties, the favourite themes of the two great masters. They enjoyed going to taverns, and were amused by watching scenes between red-faced individuals full of exuberant spirits and truculence. Their lively compositions are peopled with musicians, beggars, soldiers, gamblers, a crowd of somewhat absurd and outrageous characters.

Although a Belgian by birth, David Teniers (figs. 74–6) is one of the chief painters in this Dutch tradition. Jan Steen (fig. 125), Metsu, Gerard Dou (fig. 98), Terborch (figs. 91 and 92) and Brouwer (fig. 84) have preserved for posterity the most familiar scenes of the life they knew. Their technique was skilful and free. They did not try to invent a style, but took their measure from the subjects they treated, showing an adroitness and honesty typical of the times. Their good-humour is often coarse, but with a freedom – or licence – that is amiable and devoid of perversion; it is the counterpart of the rather austere gentleness of the bourgeois interiors. In this respect too this genre painting, as it is called, was to find an echo in the nineteenth century among painters who were also attracted by anecdote, but never succeeded in taking it beyond banal academicism. It is interesting also to note the similarity of themes, patrons and political situations – all due to the social advancement of the bourgeoisie.

Still-Life

Still-life painting came into favour in Holland and developed along lines similar to those followed in other countries. The fashion for tulips had spread like wildfire during the sixteenth century, attracting so many enthusiasts that people spoke of 'tulipomania'; they figured largely in the fine flower-pieces of the seventeenth century. Meanwhile Claesz (fig. 81) and many others were beginning to develop a slightly less stiff, less austere style, and aim at a more fragile elegance, greater movement in draughts-manship and variation in the quality of paint without, however, competing with the generous freedom of Flemish painters like Rubens or the ample decorative compositions of Desportes in France.

Portraits

Dutch portraiture has also to be considered in reference to the conditions of life in Holland. It was popular in all its forms, but always showed the same quiet decorum; and the limits of honest representation were never over-stepped even in official portraits. There was no artist who set out to rival the court painting of other lands, and what was lost in pompous display was gained in humanity.

The most splendid portraits were of groups or public bodies, each man eager to appear with all the attributes of his function. Magistrates, consta-bles or drapers are seen expanding with pride in their public capacity, and these collective portraits complete the picture of Dutch life called up by other sorts of painting. They represent the other side of the medal from the interiors and tavern scenes. But in spite of their official and even conventional character, these collective portraits are not in the least academic. On the contrary they are intensely alive, and the different likenesses are often strangely suggestive and full of psychological sig-nificance and humanity. Rembrandt and Frans Hals achieved their greatest triumphs in this domain. I need only mention *The Syndics* and *The Night Watch* (fig. 108) by the former, and *The Governors of St Elizabeth's Hospital* (fig. 87) by the latter.

Other artists, particularly van der Helst, distinguished themselves in similar subjects, which often seem to be combinations of several genres. We can admire their gifts as portraitists and their exact observation of human beings, as well as their knowledge of composition and movement, their skill in the special uses of paint required by still-life, and the lively rhythm of their poses. It is proof of the variety this theme allows that two temperaments so different, or even opposed, as Rembrandt and Frans Hals should have excelled in it.

Frans Hals (figs. 85–90)

The collection of paintings by Frans Hals in the Haarlem Museum is an extremely important one. Here one can follow the development of an art which may seem superficial and over-facile at first sight, but gradually acquires a more serious tone and culminates in two great masterpieces – the group portraits of the Governors (fig. 87), and particularly that of the Women Governors, a piece of pitiless observation in which the painter shows no desire to seduce, but states the character of each person with relentless frankness. Each brush-stroke helps to model the forms, leaving behind a mark as definite and uncompromising as a scratch by a claw. There is none of the coarseness here that we saw in his laughing *Drunkards* or dishevelled women (fig. 90) a few years earlier – nothing except the virtuosity with which he sets white against black, and makes the latter more luminous, brilliant and vibrant than bright colours. Again we see the seventeenth century foreshadowing the nineteenth, for Frans Hals was the Manet of his day – Manet at his most audacious, and with as free a technique.

Rembrandt (figs. 104–11)

As for Rembrandt, he was a marvel going beyond the limits of his time, his society, influences or subjects; he was a genius in every sense of the word, a genius in whom there is much that is inexplicable, in fact miraculous. I shall not exhaust the list of his virtues if I say that he was a very great painter in every genre, unsurpassable in landscape (figs. 110 and 111), large compositions (fig. 108) or portraits (figs. 106, 107 and 109). His technique is a constantly renewed, indefinable and mysterious triumph, although it seems always to be making use of some fortunate accident. One can analyse the technique of Velázquez, Raphael or Giotto; one can understand how the design combines with the colour, how the colour has been made to have form and density. But as one stands before some of Rembrandt's canvases, and looks at the sleeve of the young man in *The Jewish Bride*, for instance, or Saul's hands, or some of the details of the placid *The Syndics*, one is unable to understand how or why the artist has contrived, with these flickering colours, these blobs of paint glittering like precious stones, to build up so precise a form, suggest so exact a consistency and such a boundless space.

Everything about Rembrandt is miraculous, not only his painting, but also his engraving and draughtsmanship. In his drawings every line transfigures the paper on which it is traced. In a landscape without shadows or apparent contour, the bare surface of the paper above or below a traced line takes on a different quality according to whether Rembrandt wants it to represent sky or earth. Whatever the subject of a picture by Rembrandt, one always seems to be in the presence of something sacred. Protestantism had practically put an end to church painting in Holland, but Rembrandt and Rembrandt alone preserved the sacred flame, the warm radiance of the holy images.

The range of colour in seventeenth-century Dutch painting was very different from that of the sixteenth century. The bluish light suffusing Brueghel's or Patinir's landscapes vanished, leaving a countryside powdered with gold.

Rembrandt, Salomon van Ruysdael and also van Goyen painted almost in monochrome, and their desire to observe and reproduce reality did not prevent their impregnating it with their own emotions, both for the sake of harmony and so as to add something of themselves – a reflection of their own imaginations.

Their scrupulous fidelity to the limits of reality did not exclude dreams, and sometimes even gave them special prominence. Some of Jacob van Ruysdael's landscapes are permeated with anguish, with a tense, obsessional quality as if they were destined to be the setting for a drama of some sort. Some of the minor masters' interiors give one the feeling that something extraordinary – a sort of mystical act – is about to happen. There are tavern scenes whose grotesque figures in absurd attitudes seem determined to make one laugh and do not come far short of Goya's monstrosities.

With Rembrandt, the boundary between the real and the fantastic is more than usually indefinite. Some future Faust seems to be brooding in the luminous shadows from which his figures loom; and it is this fantastic element perhaps which so completely differentiates seventeenth-century Dutch art from that of nineteenth-century France. For, although Holland's landscape-painters to some extent herald the Barbizon School and English painters such as Constable, it is difficult to see any relation between them and French Impressionism.

Lastly it is noticeable that the Dutch seventeenth-century painters showed little interest in women, especially in comparison to the eighteenth century. It is not that women were unrepresented or ill-treated, but no attempt was made to flatter them, nor did the artist try to make them seductive. In Belgium, with Rubens and his followers, the position was different, but he was outside the main current. In Holland, Vermeer's tender approach to women never went beyond placid affection, and the genre paintings of the minor masters more often portray easy debauches than more refined feminine charms. As for Rembrandt, he often reveals his love for his young wife and model, Saskia, for us; his portraits of her are moving, but as free from coquetry or desire as his paintings of old women.

To sum up, woman was a theme of secondary importance to an epoch when men were most probably too preoccupied with themselves, their rights and duties, to let themselves be carried away by feminine seductiveness.

But everywhere and in all subjects manhood is emphasized with a tranquil confidence based on reason as much as on stable social conditions. If Holland does not offer us so wide a view or so complete a synthesis of ideas as the rest of Europe and its art, it is probably because geographically and politically she was at the crossroads, in process of developing her new ideas of freedom and man's ability and responsibilities. It is astonishing and admirable that her respect for moderation did not reduce her to mediocrity, astonishing and admirable that she should have produced the works of Vermeer and, above all, of Rembrandt.

France

During the seventeenth century, the opposition between the two currents which had always been present in Western painting was more defined in France than elsewhere; from now on it emerged as the conflict between the classical and baroque styles. For a long time all France's energies had been more or less consciously tending towards consolidation, and the control of contradictory elements by organization. Territorial and political unity had been built up, century by century, with a continuity that was perhaps unconscious, but impressively permanent, and in face of violent opposition. From now on France was an effective entity, instead of a potentiality or a temporary state, as she had been for so long. Today we think of her as a logical necessity, but she had to earn and win her independent status. To achieve this, a balance had to be found between the power of the monarchy, the pooling of certain material interests and the disappearance of certain rivalries; meanwhile, neighbouring states remained in a state of flux, and minor potentates wielded uncertain power without knowing which would triumph over the rest.

In France power was established in a more or less definite form; the way of life was based on that of the court, without being excessively standardized. The centralization of power involved the centralization of talent. Provincial distinctions were not to disappear, however; on the contrary, it was thanks to them that some excellent artists infused a vitality free from Parisian conventions into their own province. It is only necessary to mention the names of Rivalz in Provence, Chalette (fig. 136) in Toulouse and Nicolas Mignard in Avignon, to give an idea of the high standard of some provincial productions and their genuine originality. Even so, they established a link between Paris and the provinces – a link that was not a form of submission but a common way of thinking, just as there was now a common language.

The Académie
This notion of order and unity was crystallized around the creation of the Académie. The Académie Française had been founded by Richelieu in 1635, and was concerned among other things with the defence and consolidation of the French language. The Académie Royale de Peinture et de Sculpture was founded a few years later in 1648, in response to a more or

less analagous need, but also had an exact professional function. In this capacity it was symptomatic of social development in the seventeenth century. In Italy during the preceding century, painters had already begun to form into groups for their own financial or artistic protection, with statutes covering their rights and functions; there was even an attempt to impose aesthetic principles on them.

The difference between artist and artisan was gradually making itself felt, but in France the position of painters had hardly changed and was still subject to the general rules of their guild. In other words house-painters, as we now call them, and painters of pictures had to conform to the same regulations. When an artist was commissioned to decorate a site or a room he had to undertake the painting of doors, mouldings and fillets, as well as the composition of designs for some of the panels. The artist was obliged to accept the hierarchy of his guild, and was only allowed to work on these conditions. To get to the top of his profession, he had to go through the various stages of apprenticeship and introduction before being recognized and admitted by his 'equals', who would not necessarily be artists themselves. By arousing a spirit of independence, and insisting on the value of individualism, the Renaissance had inevitably acted against these principles. And besides, the nobility were disinclined to follow these rules when choosing men to decorate their palaces and wanted to be free to follow their own artistic preferences, so that they were always trying to evade the restrictions. They were reduced to be-stowing unusual functions on those whose talent they wanted to employ. This was why princes often gave artists the title of 'valet' or 'usher', so that they could entrust the decoration of their houses to them. Frequent conflicts were the result, because whenever possible the guild pursued any artist who tried to escape from its jurisdiction by such subterfuges.

The founding of the Académie was therefore a form of professional defence, for it gave the artists their own system of regulations, adapted to their functions and quite different from that of the artisans. It appeared to liberate artists from the control of those we would today think of as exploiters of painting but, in fact, it placed them under the more august but no less exacting protection of the King or his representatives. It soon became apparent that under the new arrangement an official aesthetic would be imposed, and work would only be given to those artists who subscribed to it. With the founding of the Académie, the possibility of academicism inevitably arose.

Academicism

Academicism, or rather a state of mind favourable to it, was not a sudden growth. The first signs had been visible during the preceding century at Fontainebleau, but it took the form of an aesthetic trend before it became a doctrine. It already very clearly involved the affirmation of the dignity of man, of which I have already spoken. It showed a leaning towards absolute values and stable principles of order and discipline, such as were then in fashion and on which the new society was founded. So that, when the Académie Royale was assured of official support and given extensive power, this was simply the regularization of an already existing state of affairs. Henceforward, there was state art, just as there was state religion, a state theatre, a royal army and national industries. Richelieu, Mazarin and, finally, Colbert were to follow in the footsteps of Francis I and Henry IV and make this new force a means of proclaiming the omnipotence of the sovereign state and its ideas, in the arts as well as in other activities.

Circumstances were favourable, and the scheme was undertaken by men capable of carrying it out. The two organizers were: Jean Baptiste Colbert who, as a minister, had the means of combining scattered activities, and Charles Le Brun, who was an artist with the necessary qualities for giving breadth to the undertaking. As head of the Académie Royale des Beaux Arts, director of the Gobelins tapestry mills and supervisor of all the decorations destined for Versailles, Le Brun had considerable power. The result of his accepting this onerous task was that a very pronounced style rapidly made its appearance and the century became known as 'the great century' or 'the century of Louis XIV', although Le Brun only took over the Gobelins in 1663, and Louis XIV had not come to the throne until 1643 and was only five years old at the time. In fact, the ideas of the seventeenth century had already been clearly defined before these two events. However, the new ideas had such a widespread effect that it is often forgotten that they were not spontaneously created, but were the inevitable conclusion of a chain of circumstances.

We must also remember that the growth of classicism – and its abnormally fossilized form, academicism – did not eliminate all other trends and there were during the seventeenth century many signs of what the eighteenth was to become.

Behind so much discussion and so many new developments there was always visible a desire to serve the truth more scrupulously, to grasp both the appearances of life and its inner significance. The fact that Poussin and other painters who had visited Rome showed a renewed interest in the art of antiquity is to be explained by the lesson they found in it – that realism and faithfulness to nature were preferable to the conventionality of the Middle Ages. This desire for truth was carried so far that, before painting a picture, Poussin often used to construct a life-size décor, and make a little model of the figures and subject inside a box, which he followed as exactly as possible. (This was also an aid to composition.) But his desire for truth was not soulless; for him 'the object of art was delight'.

However, similar intentions produced different results, and this led to rivalries.

Although the dispute between the followers of Rubens and Poussin in the Académie from 1671 to 1672 brought Philippe de Champaigne and Blanchard into violent conflict; although this was an instance of the eternal rivalry between ancient and modern, drawing and painting, or (to bring our terms up to date) classicism and baroque; and although the dispute assumed formidable proportions, this only goes to show that there were many artists who refused docilely to accept the formulae imposed on them in the name of classicism. Even Le Brun's out-and-out verdict in favour of the followers of Poussin and against those of Rubens did not extinguish the latter. We must remember that in 1666 van der Meulen had been officially commissioned to paint the important events of the century, its famous battles in particular, and that his art was much closer to Rubens than Poussin and clearly anticipated the eighteenth century. Le Brun himself, concerned as he was to glorify official pomp, had very little of Poussin's austerity and, to some extent, followed the tradition set by Rubens's vast decorations celebrating the reign of Henry IV and Marie de' Medici.

From all this one may conclude that the chief trends in art are controlled not by a certain way of thinking or a certain philosophy alone, but largely by new social conditions, and especially by political conditions making it possible for art to become one of the essential activities of a nation. So that, rather than analyse the work of each individual painter, it seems more effective, more conclusive a way of summing up French seventeenth-century art, to study the painters' relation to their themes, and try to understand in what way they translated and expressed the needs of society. A work of art was no longer a simple image created to honour the Church or some great nobleman; it was the product of public or private life, it reflected the thoughts of both creator and owner. It was, therefore, an illustration of the times and can be consulted as such. Before discovering what the works are and in what circumstances they were painted, it may perhaps be useful to find out why and for whom they were carried out and what their place was in the productive activity of the period. It will be interesting to see what each of these themes will yield, taken separately.

Portraiture

It is in portraiture that we are most likely to find a clue to the parallel developments in thought and social conditions, because a portrait is more closely linked than any other work with the lives of the men who have commissioned and carried it out. More than any other theme it revealed the desire to dedicate specialized skill to the service of the ruling power, even when directed by personal vanity. A portrait was now more than ever expected to depict a man in his public capacity.

It was also through portraiture that the sixteenth and seventeenth centuries were linked. During the French Renaissance some of the greatest painters of the day had been famous for their drawings in silver-point, lead pencil or sanguine, and this successful activity continued for some years. There were dynasties of painters, or sometimes groups of craftsmen sharing a family tradition. These were attached either to the Royal Family or to some great nobleman and used to carry out innumerable portraits of the same person to be given as presents. In fact, they played the part now taken by photographers, and their highly specialized technique was handed on from father to son. The Clouet family was perhaps the most famous and gifted in this line, but they do not go beyond the sixteenth century, whereas the Dumonstier, Bunel and Quesnel dynasties persisted into the first half of the seventeenth. They maintained the high prestige of the family and official portrait combined, before the appearance of court portraiture proper, in all its splendour, as it was exemplified by Le Brun under Louis XIV.

The Pourbus family represent a transition period in which the sitter's pose was more carefully studied and treated with less constraint, showing kinship with Rubens. After them, more importance was given to fine clothes.

As the art of portrait-painting became more specialized, the artists practising it developed a faithfulness to outward appearances which was a form of stylization and differed from the attention to detail typical of French or Flemish Gothic. But, however official the portraits might be, they did not tend to become anonymous, for they aimed at a synthesis of the sitter's personal characteristics. Faithful representation was no longer enough; a more difficult, intellectual feat of understanding was required of the painter. Before the advent of Le Brun, and during his reign, there was room for a number of portraitists whom we shall find also painting large compositions, and who enriched their century with a brilliant gallery of likenesses representing an evolving society.

In a parallel but complementary stream, we find a trend towards extreme austerity, a mood of silent, self-absorbed meditation. The Le Nain brothers (Antoine and Louis) and Philippe de Champaigne (fig. 160) are admirable examples of this trend. I might add Nicolas Poussin, except that he was far from prolific in portraiture; the few examples we have of his work, particularly his self-portrait (fig. 158), deserve to be ranked among the most expressive of the period. The most memorable of Philippe de Champaigne's portraits are those of the Port-Royal nuns; they bear the impress of his seriousness, of an inner life, and a stern concentration that almost seems like lack of feeling. As for the Le Nain brothers, their rustic scenes are family portraits (figs. 137–40), ennobling humble life by the careful painting of faces and the seriousness of poses. Mathieu, the youngest of the brothers, succeeded in avoiding this austerity and was attracted by court portraiture. But he was much younger than his brothers, and almost seemed to belong to another generation.

Classical ideals imposed great restraints on all these painters, forbidding any excess – particularly the fanciful and theatrical poses which were to reappear attractively in the eighteenth century and dramatically in the nineteenth. Seventeenth-century portraiture showed the limits insisted on by an official discipline; it did not necessarily exclude a human approach, but fortified it with respect for good manners and a sort of modesty.

Court portraits were the embodiment of official art, particularly those of Le Brun, who understood and ministered perfectly to Louis XIV's ambition. He put his sense of grandeur at the service of the King, undertaking the most diverse subjects and employing every artistic technique available at the time, including the invention of designs for the decorations and silverware of the royal palaces. Mignard's work (fig. 171) is lacking in force compared to his. He had the same qualities and the same desire to express the grandeur of his times; he knew how to produce court art that was not banal, but he can hardly be said to have risen above this level. He lacked Le Brun's personal note, which gave originality even to works that were painted solely to order. After Le Brun, Rigaud (fig. 175) was appointed official court painter and received commissions for innumerable portraits. He had neither Philippe de Champaigne's austerity nor Le Brun's breadth of treatment; his work was pleasant without being informal and, even in his pompous moods, his academicism seems to point towards less severity of style. This trend became more definite with Largillière, who is often classed among eighteenth-century painters, although a large part of his work was done in the seventeenth, and who shows an almost insensible transition between the pompous pride of Louis XIV and the futile elegance of Louis XV.

The Choice of Subjects

There was, of course, a close relationship between painters and the now all-powerful court. They largely depended on it for their livelihood and for commissions for paintings, and some were even lodged in the Louvre. The result was a great change in the choice of subjects. Artists were invited to glorify the reigning power now controlling all the nation's activities. The large compositions they were commissioned to paint were destined to ornament the various palaces. They must therefore celebrate the history of the regime and commemorate victories and conquests; even allegories must have a social and political meaning. Religious painting retired into the shade. The Church was no longer the chief client to be satisfied, and religious subjects were less important than battle-pieces. Besides, it was an age of grandeur rather than drama; enthusiasm was aroused by achievement, and humility was out of favour. Historical painters began to have unprecedented success; the halls of châteaux were decorated with representations of political and historical events or pagan allegories gratifying the new taste for fable and fantasy. This predilection for imaginative realism was a heritage from Italy; though reminiscent of the most splendid achievements of the preceding centuries on the other side of the Alps, it was carried out in a quite different spirit, according to the new rules and in a style embodying the French aesthetic stand-point.

Italian Influence

Italian influence had already been much in evidence at the beginning of the century, because of the decorations at Fontainebleau. Every monarch in turn had for the last century added some embellishment to this superb château, in token of his presence and as an original imprint of the times. The last group of great decorators contained only a few Italians; the French had mastered the necessary technique sufficiently to take control. Fontainebleau prepared the way for the triumphant richness of Versailles. Toussaint Dubreuil, Amboise Dubois, and more especially Freminet were the last representatives of this French Renaissance known as the Fontainebleau School and the first to show signs of the new style. They had already discovered how to extract the essence of the national character, and thus they directly paved the way for the classicism which was to be the most typical creation of the seventeenth century – so essential to the spirit of the age that it would never disappear again.

Poussin (figs. 153–9)

Most French painters went to Italy to study their art, sometimes remaining there for several years; and this custom continued for a long while. Poussin's case is typical, for he spent most of his life in Rome. In spite of the commissions he received from the King of France and the brilliant posts offered him, he was only in Paris from 1640 to 1642, preferring to return to Rome, where he remained till his death

Although he lived so long in Italy and did most of his work there, Poussin's influence in France was great, and it was his art, his ideas and his principles that were set up in opposition to Rubens's in the disputes between members of the Académie Royale de Peinture et de Sculpture and the often very violent controversies that enlivened the century. He also had an adversary in Simon Vouet (fig. 174), born a few years earlier (Vouet was born in 1590 and Poussin in 1594), who had achieved considerable fame while Poussin was still struggling and insecure. It was with some bitterness that Simon Vouet watched the ascent of this new star – the rival painter he rightly felt was soon going to eclipse him.

Claude Lorrain (figs. 164–8), Blanchard (fig. 147) and Valentin (fig. 169)
There were also a whole group of painters, all born within a few years of each other – Claude Gellée, known as Lorrain, 1600; Blanchard, 1600, Valentin, c 1594 – all of whom spent longer or shorter periods in Italy; they formed the nucleus of a very solid French School, personal both in inspiration and style, in spite of the influences they were subjected to and accepted, ranging from Raphael to Caravaggio, and thus they prepared for the birth of classicism at the same time that they heralded the romanticism of the future.

These painters gave as much attention to the themes of their interiors (or easel-paintings, as they are now called) as to those of their large compositions, mythological scenes or representations of contemporary life; they never allowed them to become anecdotic and, in spite of their small size, kept to the rules of composition as strictly as in their large murals.

Italian Influence Diminishes
So, between 1580 and 1610, the great international stars went off to Italy, and France saw the birth of the men who were to take their place. Some of this new generation were less profoundly affected by Italian influences, or even escaped them altogether. Among these were the Le Nain brothers (born 1588, 1593 and 1607) (figs. 137–41), Philippe de Champaigne (1602) (figs. 160–3), the Mignard brothers (1606 and 1612) (Pierre, fig. 171) and Georges de la Tour (1593) (figs. 142–6). A few of them showed traces of Caravaggism, but they made use of it rather than submitted to it, and turned it into a personal form of expression. So that, quite early in the seventeenth century, French painting found its own style, a style in conformity with the elegant but stern disciplines of court etiquette. This first group was followed by another which developed this style and gave it breadth and power; Le Brun (1619) (fig. 150) was the most gifted, and Sébastien Bourdon (figs. 172 and 173) the most successful in accommodating his talents to different formulae, while Le Sueur (born in 1617) (fig. 151) remained the most faithful to Poussin's principles.

Historical Painting
Louis XIV's brilliant reign required more of its painters than portraits recording the features of famous people, or mythology to honour their virtues. The more the King's power increased, the longer his reign lasted and the wider his domains spread, the greater became the need to commemorate the outstanding events of the age. The historical painters who

were given this task became conspicuously important. I have said that van der Meulen was commissioned to paint the most famous battles and victories of the reign; other artists also provided vigorous examples of this genre, such as Courtois, known as Le Bourguignon, and Parrocel. They adapted their style to their subjects; they delighted in galloping horses, flying plumes, cavalry charges careering over vast landscapes, and smoking cannons, but never lost the characteristic elegance which was to give way to drama in the nineteenth century. They discovered poetry in motion, and thus, on the pretext of realism, were serving the cause of romanticism, for they already showed the technical skill, nervous draughtsmanship, and rapid and expressive brushwork that were to make Delacroix a great master two centuries later. But in his hands, these gifts expressed deep passion, instead of the disciplined elegance of the court of Louis XIV.

Georges de la Tour (figs. 142–6)

These representations of contemporary historical events were far removed from the realism of Caravaggio's followers, who had turned rather towards ideal constructions and a static magic such as is forcefully embodied in the work of Georges de la Tour. No one understood better than he how to make use of back-lighting, extract intense poetic feeling from immobility, or use light to give density to forms while surrounding them with a firm outline filled in with large expanses of flat, almost unmodelled colour.

Still-Life

A similar technique and poetical quality are to be found in many of the still-lifes, especially Baugin's (fig. 134), which have much in common with those of painters of the Spanish school such as Zurbarán, Velázquez and Cotán. During the second half of the century, still-life grew freer and began to develop along more pleasing lines, forecasting the eighteenth century. Desportes was a notable example.

Landscape Painting: Claude Lorrain and Nicolas Poussin

French seventeenth-century art seems thus to have been concerned almost entirely with current reality and with paying homage to the great ones of the period and their exploits. When it abandoned this function, it devoted itself to representing familiar domestic scenes. However, there is one painter who did not conform to this definition, though he was very much in sympathy with his epoch: this was Claude Gellée, known as Lorrain. His admiration for Italy, where he lived for most of his long life, is shown less in his technique than in the inspiration he found there. He did not so much try to imitate the marvellous landscapes in which he had lived as use them to reconstruct the fairyland of the ancient world and its legends. Claude Lorrain (figs. 164–8) leads us along from one dream to another, with vistas of palaces reflected in water marbled by the setting sun. By evoking pagan divinities, he became a great landscape-painter; one might even say that he and Poussin were the two greatest French landscape-painters of their age, and two of the greatest of all time. These two artists were the authors of a true renaissance of French landscape-painting, of a landscape that was dramatic, carefully composed, with parallel planes leading into the far distance as in an effective theatrical décor.

The second half of the seventeenth century saw the appearance of painters heralding the eighteenth century, who were transitional between the pomposity of court painting and the more pleasing, relaxed art of the Regency and the reign of Louis XV. Rigaud and particularly Largillière illustrate this stage in portraiture, Desportes in still-life and Parrocel in historical painting. There was a return too to the dynasties of painters that had been a feature of the sixteenth century. The van Loo, Coypel, Boullongue and Parrocel families – fathers, sons, nephews and cousins – formed the links in a chain which smoothly united one century with the next.

To sum up, it was during the seventeenth century that French art developed its distinctive character. It is possible to reduce the list of painters to a few names as in the case of Spain; Poussin, Le Brun, Claude Lorrain, Georges de la Tour, Philippe de Champaigne, the Le Nain brothers, Mignard and van der Meulen sufficiently evoke the different aspects of the century. They were less isolated than the great Spanish masters. In fact, to take their true measure, one must see them surrounded and followed by less famous artists, whose existence they justify.

1 Annibale Carracci

2 Annibale Carracci

3 Caravaggio

4 Caravaggio

5 Caravaggio

6 Caravaggio

7 Caravaggio

8 Domenico Fetti

9 Carlo Saraceni

10 Domenichino

11 Guido Reni

12   Orazio Gentileschi

13 Francesco Albani

14 Evaristo Baschenis

15 Pietro da Cortona

16 Pietro da Cortona

17 Luca Giordano

18 Guercino

19 Andrea del Pozzo

20 Juan Pantoja de la Cruz

21 Juan Sánchez Cotán

22 Juan Bautista Mayno

23 Francisco de Herrera

24 Jusepe de Ribera

25 Jusepe de Ribera

26 Jusepe de Ribera

27   Jusepe de Ribera

28 Velázquez

29   Velázquez

30 Velázquez

31 Velázquez

32   Velázquez

33 Velázquez

34 Velázquez

35   Velázquez

36 Bartolomé Esteban Murillo

37   Bartolomé Esteban Murillo

38   Bartolomé Esteban Murillo

39 Francisco de Zurbarán

40   **Francisco de Zurbarán**

41 Francisco de Zurbarán

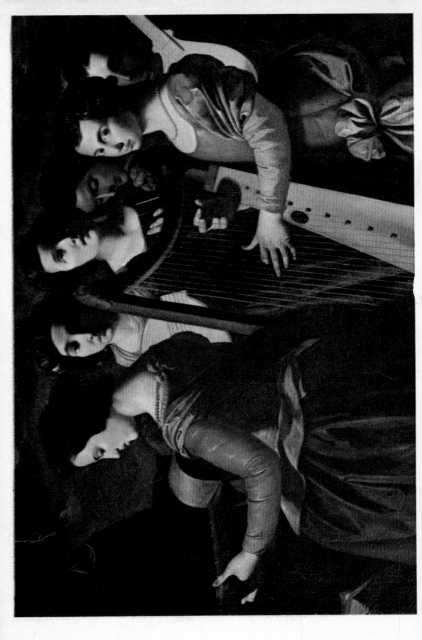

42 Francisco de Zurbarán

43 Francisco de Zurbarán

44 Francisco de Zurbarán

45 Francisco de Zurbarán

46 Juan de Váldes Leal

47 Juan de Váldes Leal

48 Juan Carreño de Miranda

49 Juan Rizi

50　Jean Daret

51 Louis Finson

52   Caspar de Crayer

53 Jan Fyt

54 Paul de Vos

55　Jacob Jordaens

56 Jacob Jordaens

57 Jan Brueghel

58 Jan Brueghel

59   Jan Brueghel

60 Jan Brueghel

61　Jan Brueghel

62 Jan Brueghel

63   Peter Paul Rubens

64   Peter Paul Rubens

65   Peter Paul Rubens

66   Peter Paul Rubens

67   Peter Paul Rubens

68   Peter Paul Rubens

69   Peter Paul Rubens

70   Peter Paul Rubens

1 Anthonie van Dijck / Anthony van Dyck

72 Anthonie van Dijck / Anthony van Dyck

73 Anthonie van Dijck / Anthony van Dyck

74 David Teniers II

75 David Teniers II

76 David Teniers II

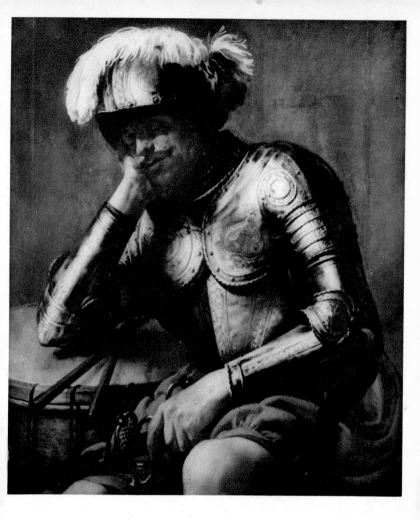

77   Hendrick Terbrugghen

78 Roeland Savery

79 Frans Snyders

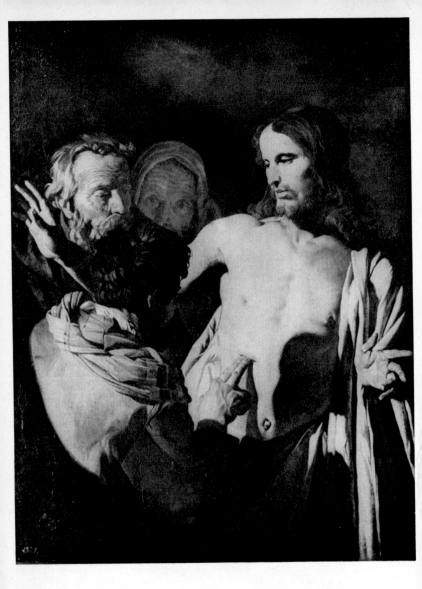

80   Gerard van Honthorst

82   Hercules Seghers

83　Hercules Seghers

84   Adriaen Brouwer

85 Frans Hals

86 Frans Hals

87 Frans Hals

88 Frans Hals

89 Frans Hals

90 Frans Hals

91 Gerard Terborch

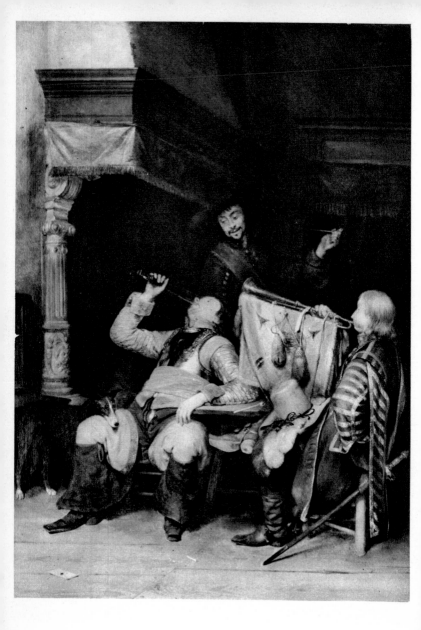

92 Gerard Terborch

93 Jan van Goyen

94   Jan van Goyen

95 Carel Fabritius

96 Pieter Saenredam

97   Paulus Potter

98 Gerard Dou

99 Jan Davidsz de Heem

100   Jacob van Ruysdael

101 Jacob van Ruysdael

102 Hendrick Avercamp

103 Gabriel Metsu

105 Rembrandt

106 Rembrandt

107 Rembrandt

109 Rembrandt

110 Rembrandt

111   Rembrandt

112   Meindert Hobbema

13   Meindert Hobbema

114 Jan Vermeer van Delft

15　Jan Vermeer van Delft

116   Jan Vermeer van Delft

117　Jan Vermeer van Delft

118   Jan Vermeer van Delft

119 Jan Vermeer van Delft

120 Albert Cuyp

121 Adriaen van de Velde

122 Karel Dujardin

123   Adriaen van Ostade

124 Frans Post

125 Jan Steen

126 Juriaen van Streeck

127 Jan van de Capelle

128   Frans van Mieris

130   Pieter de Hoogh

31 Jan van der Heyden

132 Philips de Koninck

33   Adam Elsheimer

134 André Baugin

135   L. Linard

VATIBVS · HÎC · FLORES · DANT · PRÆSIDE
APOLLINE · MVSÆ
ESTQVE · IDEM PICTO · CV̄ PRÆSIDE
VERVS · APOLLO ·

136 Jean Chalette

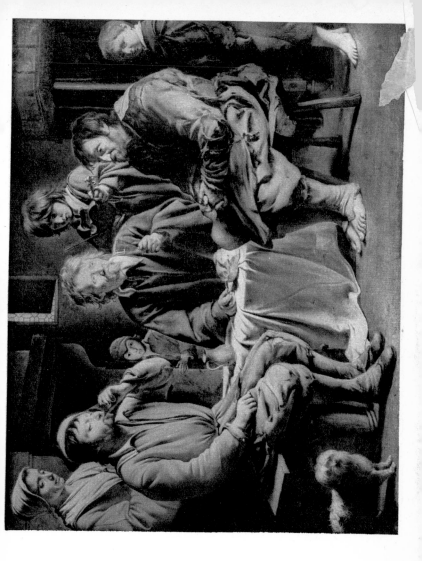

137 Louis Le Nain

138 Louis Le Nain

139 Mathieu Le Nain

140 Mathieu Le Nain

141   Antoine Le Nain

142   Georges de la Tour

143 Georges de la Tour

144 Georges de la Tour

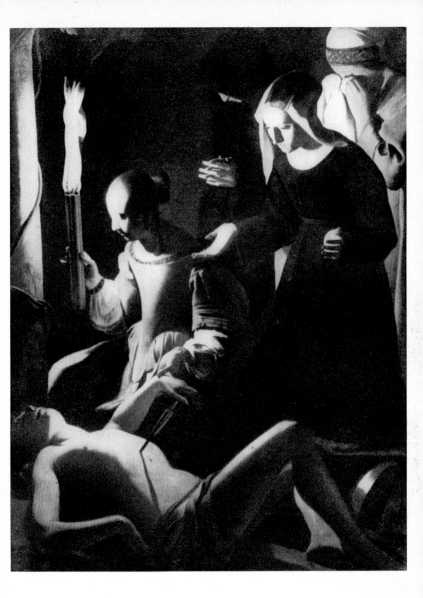

145 Georges de la Tour

146   Georges de la Tour

147 Jacques Blanchard

148   Jean Tassel

149 Antoine Durand

150 Charles Le Brun

151   Eustache Le Sueur

152 Jacques Courtois

153   Nicolas Poussin

154　Nicolas Poussin

155 Nicolas Poussin

156   Nicolas Poussin

157   Nicolas Poussin

158 Nicolas Poussin

159 Nicolas Poussin

160 Philippe de Champaigne

161 Philippe de Champaigne

162 Philippe de Champaigne

163   Philippe de Champaigne

164   Claude Lorrain

165   Claude Lorrain

166   Claude Lorrain

167 Claude Lorrain

168 Claude Lorrain

169   Valentin de Boulogne

170   Nicolas Tournier

171 Pierre Mignard

172 Sébastien Bourdon

173　Sébastien Bourdon

174 Simon Vouet

175   Hyacinthe Rigaud

176   Henri Testelin

Biographical Notes

Biographical Notes

Albani, Francesco. Italian painter. Born in Bologna in 1578, died there in 1660. Highly esteemed in his time for his mythological pictures and decorative schemes, which foreshadow eighteenth-century taste and practice, and for his religious works (*fig. 13*)

Avercamp, Hendrick. Dutch painter. Born in Amsterdam in 1585, died in Kampen in 1634. Well known painter of winter landscapes; he produced many works in oils, and a long series of drawings, often coloured, also of winter scenes. Noticeably influenced by van Coninxloo and Brueghel the Elder (*fig. 102*)

Baschenis, Evaristo. Italian painter. Born in Bergamo in 1607, died there in 1677. Painter of still-life and musical instruments (*fig. 14*)

Baugin, André. French painter of still-life. Probably born in the 1590s. Very little is known about him, but his few surviving works suggest a knowledge of the Caravaggesque style. In the past he has sometimes been confused with Lubin Baugin (*fig. 134*)

Blanchard, Jacques. French painter. Born in Paris in 1600, died there in 1638. Working in Rome and Venice, he came under the influence of sixteenth-century masters. He was nicknamed 'the French Titian' (*fig. 147*)

Bourdon, Sébastien. French painter. Born in Montpellier in 1616, died in Paris in 1671. Superintendent of the Académie Royale. In Rome 1634–7. At first influenced by the Bamboccianti, Claude, Poussin and Castiglione, he turned to an increasingly Poussinesque idiom (*figs. 172 and 173*)

Brouwer, Adriaen. Flemish-Dutch painter. Born in Oudenaerde in 1605/6, died in Antwerp in 1638. Landscape painter and specialist in brilliantly painted peasant genre, lewd in tone. A pupil of Frans Hals at Haarlem, he exercised, in his turn, a considerable influence upon other Dutch painters of genre pieces, among them van Ostade and Teniers (*fig. 84*)

Brueghel (Bruegel), Jan (Velvet Brueghel) Flemish painter. Born in Brussels in 1568, died in Antwerp in 1625. Son of Pieter Brueghel the Elder (Peasant Brueghel). Influenced by Coninxloo and Bril, he developed as a landscape and flower painter of the first order. Worked as an assistant in Rubens's studio (*figs. 57–62*)

Capelle, Jan van de. Dutch painter. Born in Amsterdam in 1623/5, died there in 1679. Well known for his sea pieces with shipping, usually calm in mood; he also painted winter landscapes somewhat reminiscent of van der Neer (*fig. 127*)

Caravaggio, Michelangelo (Merisi) da. Italian painter. Born in Caravaggio in 1573, died in Porto d'Ercole in 1610. At the close of the century that bore the impress of academic mannerism, he evolved a style of great realism, with strong effects of light and shade; it was dramatic, forceful, earthy – and revolutionary. Painters like Finson, Vouet, Terbrugghen and Honthorst were influenced by Caravaggio's naturalism, and these artists carried the new view further in their own countries to Le Nain, de la Tour, Rembrandt and Vermeer. Caravaggio's creations roused violent opposition in Italy, and his unconventional treatment of religious iconography brought forth several charges of impiety. From 1606–10 he led a roving existence in the south of Italy and in Malta (*figs. 3–7*)

Carracci, Annibale. Italian painter. Born in Bologna in 1560, died in Rome in 1609. He evolved a renewed and reinvigorated classical style, based on a study of the great sixteenth-century masters. His academy, which he founded together with his cousin Ludovico (1555–1619) and his brother Agostino (1557–1602) had much influence and guided the development of such painters as Guido Reni, Domenichino and Guercino. Annibale's most important work was the very influential Farnese Gallery decorations in the Palazzo Farnese, Rome (*figs. 1 and 2*)

Carreño de Miranda, Juan. Spanish painter. Born in Avilés in 1614, died in Madrid in 1685. Court painter. Influenced by Rubens and others. Produced portraits and altar-pieces (*fig. 48*)

Chalette, Jean. French painter. Born in Troyes in 1581, died in Toulouse in 1643. One of the best portrait painters of his time (*fig. 136*)

Champaigne (Champagne), Philippe de. French painter. Born in Brussels in 1602, died in Paris in 1674. At first influenced by a modified form of Rubensian baroque, he evolved in France a more classical manner. His Flemish descent in combination with French spiritual values resulted in a profound conception of, and psychological approach to, his themes, thus placing his portraits and religious paintings in the highest rank of French art in the seventeenth century. Champaigne belonged to the Jansenists of Port-Royal (*figs. 160–3*)

Claesz, Pieter. Netherlandish painter. Born in Burgsteinfurt in 1597/8, died in Haarlem in 1661. Painter of still-life (*fig. 81*)

Cortona, Pietro da (Pietro Berrettini). Italian painter and architect. Born in Cortona in 1596, died in Rome in 1669. He was one of the creators of the High Baroque style. His most important painting is the large, rich and exuberant ceiling fresco in the Palazzo Barberini, Rome (*figs. 15 and 16*)

Cotán, Juan Sánchez. Spanish painter. Born in Orgaz in 1561, died in Granada in 1627. Prominent painter of still-life, he later chose subjects of a religious nature as well (*fig. 21*)

Courtois, Jacques (Giacomo Cortese). (Le Bourguignon). Franco-Italian painter. Born in Saint-Hippolyte in 1621. By c 1640 in Rome where he died in 1675. Painter of battle scenes, in a style influenced by Cerquozzi and Rosa (*fig. 152*)

Crayer, Caspar (Jasper) de. Flemish painter. Born in Antwerp in 1582, died in Ghent in 1669. Well acquainted with Rubens and van Dyck and under the influence of both. Painted almost exclusively religious scenes for churches, but also some portraits. He ran a large studio on the lines of Rubens's (*fig. 52*)

Cuyp (Cuijp), Albert. Dutch landscape painter. Born in Dordrecht in 1620, died there in 1691. Worked under the influence of Salomon van Ruysdael and Jan van Goyen, but later came under the spell of Italianizing artists such as Berchem, painting his most typical works in a sun-drenched, idealized idiom that led him to be dubbed 'the Dutch Claude' (*fig. 120*)

Daret, Jean. Flemish painter. Born in Brussels in 1613, died in Aix-en-Provence in 1668. He worked in

Bologna for some years where he benefited from Guido Reni's and other painters' art. The influence of Guercino is noticeable as well. His work includes altar-pieces for churches in southern France, as well as portraits and engravings. Settled at Aix in 1637 (*fig. 50*)

Domenichino, (Domenico Zampieri). Italian painter. Born in Bologna in 1581, died in Naples in 1641. Pupil of Ludovico Carracci. An exponent of baroque classicism in its severe form. He influenced Poussin, and his landscapes had an impact on Claude's work in the late 1640s. He produced frescoes, altar-pieces, small devotional pictures and portraits (*fig. 10*)

Dou, Gerard. Dutch painter. Born in Leyden in 1613, died there in 1675. Pupil of Rembrandt, whose early style formed the basis for his own small-scale genre scenes. These he painted in an increasingly meticulous idiom that brought him fame, wealth and the patronage of Queen Christina of Sweden (*fig. 98*)

Dujardin, Karel. Dutch painter. Born in Amsterdam in 1621/2 (?), died in Venice in 1678. Painted idealized, Italianate landscapes in a style influenced by Berchem. He also produced portraits and religious pieces, and a handful of genre scenes and classical subjects (*fig. 122*)

Durand, Antoine. French painter who worked 1645–63 in Toulouse. Painted portraits and historical pictures. Appointed municipal painter of Toulouse. Studied under Jean Chalette (*fig. 149*)

Dyck, Sir Anthony van (Anthonie van Dijck). Flemish painter and engraver. Born in Antwerp in 1599, died in London in 1641. A very precocious artist, he was early associated with Rubens, whose style and range of subject matter he took over, though he came to concentrate on portraits in Italy, where he worked 1622–7, in Antwerp and, finally, in England, the centre of his activities from 1632 until his death. Van Dyck's aristocratic style, influenced by Titian, was ideally suited to the sensitive collector, Charles I, and he has left us an unforgettable image of the Caroline Court in all its glamorous and poignant isolation from reality. His influence on later European painting was very considerable (*figs. 71–3*)

Elsheimer, Adam. German painter. Born in Frankfurt in 1578, died in Rome in 1610. The influence of the Venetian School and Caravaggio was early apparent in his romantic conceptions. In Rome he became friendly with Rubens and Lastman, the teacher of Rembrandt. With his romantic, often nocturnal landscapes which already bear the mark of the baroque style, he exercised an influence upon Claude (*fig. 133*)

Fabritius, Carel. Dutch painter. Born in Amsterdam in 1622, killed in Delft in 1654. Probably the most important pupil of Rembrandt. In his short life he created a vigorous style with bold light effects that influenced Vermeer, de Hoogh and Emanuel de Witte (*fig. 95*)

Fetti (Feti), Domenico. Italian painter. Born in Rome in 1589, died in Venice in 1624. Painted, under the influence of Caravaggio, the Venetians and Rubens, small-scale pictures, often of parables, in a broadly handled and richly coloured style (*fig. 8*)

Finson (Finsonius/Vinson), Louis (Ludovicus). Flemish painter. Born in Bruges before 1580, died in Amsterdam *c* 1618. He worked in Provence and in Naples in a style influenced by Caravaggio and his followers (*fig. 51*)

Fyt, Jan. Flemish painter and engraver. Born in Antwerp in 1611, died there in 1661. Painter of still-life and also of hunting and animal scenes. He was a pupil of Snyders (*fig. 53*)

Gentileschi, Orazio (Lomi). Italian painter. Born in Pisa in 1563, died in London in 1647(?). He worked in Rome moulding himself after the pattern of Caravaggio and Elsheimer. By 1626 he had settled in England, where he became court painter to Charles I (*fig. 12*)

Giordano, Luca. Italian painter. Born in Naples in 1632, died there in 1705. He left a large oeuvre behind which shows that he imitated the style of a number of masters – Ribera, Veronese, Titian, Caravaggio, Rembrandt and Rubens (*fig. 17*)

Goyen, Jan van. Dutch landscape painter. Born in Leyden in 1596, died in The Hague in 1656. Pupil of Esaias van der Velde. An important exponent of the new tonal landscape style of which he was one of the founders (*figs. 93 and 94*)

Guercino (Giovanni Francesco Barbieri). Italian painter. Born near Bologna in 1591, died there in 1666. Noticeably influenced by Caravaggio and Guido Reni. Painted genre pieces, historical and biblical scenes. His earlier works are the more vigorous; he later succumbed to a more classical, calmer mode of expression (*fig. 18*)

Hals, Frans. Dutch portrait painter. Born in Antwerp *c* 1580, died in Haarlem in 1666. Pupil of Karel van Mander; a member of the so-called 'School of Haarlem' which produced many famous artists (Molenaer, van Ostade, van Ruysdael). A fine portrait painter and co-founder of a purely Dutch school of painting unaffected by Italian influence. Hals caught in his paintings the 'moment' while, at the same time, his psychological intuition enabled him to portray specific characters (as, for example, the Governors of St Elizabeth's Hospital and Hille Bobbe). He also painted genre pieces (*figs. 85–90*)

Heem, Jan Davidsz de. Dutch painter. Born in Utrecht in 1606, died in Antwerp in 1683/4. One of the most prominent Dutch painters of still-life with the characteristic motif of fruits and flowers (*fig. 99*)

Herrera, Francisco de (el Viejo – the Elder). Spanish painter. Born in Seville *c* 1576, died in Madrid in 1656. Well known for his genre pieces, he also painted religious and mythologi-

cal scenes, and was active as an engraver (*fig. 23*)

Heyden, Jan van der. Dutch painter. Born in Gorinchen in 1637, died in Amsterdam in 1712. Important painter of townscapes and architectural subjects. Besides painting, he was also active on projects to improve street lighting and fire-fighting (*fig. 131*)

Hobbema, Meindert. Dutch painter. Born in Amsterdam in 1638, died there in 1709. Pupil and friend of Jacob van Ruysdael and, like his master, one of the most prominent representatives of Dutch landscape painting. He specialized in woodland scenes. After 1668 he painted very little (*figs. 112 and 113*)

Honthorst, Gerard van. Dutch painter. Born in Utrecht in 1590, died there in 1656. Worked under the strong influence of Caravaggio, whose chiaroscuro he developed in his own individual fashion. He painted in Italy (*c* 1610–20), in England (1627–8) and for the Danish Court. He was one of the few Dutch painters of the first half of the century who enjoyed a European reputation. Large allegorical and historical paintings bear his signature, but he is better known for his intimate groups of card players and musicians lit by a torch or a candle (*fig. 80*)

Hoogh (Hooch), Pieter de. Dutch genre painter. Born in Rotterdam in 1629, died in Amsterdam after 1684(?). As a painter of interiors he ranks highest among the Dutch seventeenth-century masters. Pupil of Nicolaes Berchem and influenced by Fabritius and Vermeer (*figs. 129 and 130*)

Jordaens, Jacob. Flemish painter. Born in Antwerp in 1593, died there in 1678. He worked for a time as Rubens's assistant, and was influenced by his master's rich and painterly style, though his own work usually tends to be cruder in form, brighter in colour and more vulgar in its over-all effects. He painted a wide range of subject matter, but is famous for his large and rowdy genre scenes (*figs. 55 and 56*)

Koninck, Philips de. Dutch painter. Born in Amsterdam in 1619, died there in 1688. Strongly influenced by Rembrandt. Painted genre pieces and portraits, but it is on the strength of his panoramic landscapes that he is today regarded as one of the greatest Dutch painters of the seventeenth century (*fig. 132*)

Le Brun, Charles. French painter. Born in Paris in 1619, died there in 1690. He was trained by Vouet and also studied in Rome. As virtual dictator of the arts in France (after 1661), he was responsible for the entire decoration of Versailles and other royal properties (Marly, etc.) As a painter, he veered towards a grand, rhetorical form of classicism, ideally suited to Louis XIV's form of visual propaganda (*fig. 150*)

Le Nain. French painters.

Antoine, born in Laon in 1588, died in Paris in 1648. Painter of portraits and genre pieces (*fig. 141*)

Louis, born in Laon in 1593, died in Paris in 1648. Painter of genre pieces and religious scenes in a subdued colour key (*figs. 137 and 138*)

Mathieu, born in Laon in 1607, died in Paris in 1677. Genre painter (*figs. 139 and 140*). In the three Le Nains the influence of the Dutch genre painters and of Caravaggio is unmistakable. The three worked together in the same studio and it is hardly possible to discern one from the other as to artistic conception and technique.

Le Sueur (Lesueur), Eustache. French painter. Born in Paris in 1617, died there in 1655. Painter of religious, biblical and mythological subjects. Pupil of Vouet and influenced by the Renaissance painters and Poussin's classicism (*fig. 151*)

Linard, L. French painter. Worked in Paris mainly as a painter of still-life (*fig. 135*)

Lorrain, Claude. French painter. Born in Nancy in 1600, died in Rome in 1682. By 1627 Lorrain had settled for good in Rome, where he created, under the influence of Bril, Elsheimer and Tassi, a form of classical landscape with appropriate narrative figures from mythology and the Bible. The delicate Arcadian mood of his mature paintings is sustained by a combination of rigorous formal construction, further influenced by Domenichino and Poussin, and an acute observation of nature, recorded in hundreds of brilliant drawings (*figs. 164–8*)

Mayno, Juan Bautista. Italian-Spanish painter. Born in Lombardy *c* 1569, died in Madrid in 1649. Perhaps a pupil of Caravaggio; at all events influenced by him as well as by El Greco and Ribera (*fig. 22*)

Metsu, Gabriel. Dutch painter. Born in Leyden in 1629, died in Amsterdam in 1667. Prominent painter of genre scenes, which are notable for their rich atmosphere. Influenced by Rembrandt and Gerard Dou, who was, perhaps, his teacher (*fig. 103*)

Mieris, Frans van (the Elder). Dutch painter. Born in Leyden in 1635, died there in 1681. Important genre painter. A pupil of Gerard Dou. In his rendering of textures and fabrics and picturesque details he equals the art of Terborch, though his insistence on polish and refinement are characteristic of the decadent phase of Dutch painting (*fig. 128*)

Mignard, Pierre. French painter. Born in Troyes in 1612, died in Paris in 1695. Active as a painter of decorative schemes (of which most have disappeared) and as a court and society portrait painter. He studied under Vouet and was influenced by Correggio and seventeenth-century Bolognese painting (*fig. 171*)

Murillo, Bartolomé Esteban. Spanish painter. Born in Seville in 1617, died there in 1682. Most famous painter of the Spanish baroque style. Painted genre scenes, portraits and – most important – religious works which are among the most effective and typical examples of seventeenth-century Baroque, Catholic art. He developed under the influence of his fellow-countrymen Ribera and Velázquez, but also under that of van Dyck and Rubens (*figs. 36–8*)

Ostade, Adriaen van. Dutch painter. Born in Haarlem in 1610, died there in 1685. He is said to have studied with Hals, but this is doubtful. What is more certain and probable is an apprenticeship with Brouwer, whose influence is clear. In the 1640s he came under the influence of Rembrandt's chiaroscuro technique (*fig. 123*).

Pantoja de la Cruz, Juan. Spanish portrait painter. Born in Valladolid in 1553, died in Madrid in 1608. Court painter to Philip II and Philip III. Painter of portraits and religious subjects in the mannerist style. Influenced in the hieratic treatment of costume and accessories by his master, Coello (*fig. 20*)

Post, Frans. Dutch painter. Born in Leyden *c* 1612, died in Haarlem in 1680. Painted exotic Brazilian landscapes based on his experiences in the service of Prince Jan Maurits of Nassau (The Brazilian), in Brazil (1637–44) (*fig. 124*)

Potter, Paulus. Dutch painter of animals in landscape. Born in Enkhuizen in 1625, died in Amsterdam in 1654. He also made etchings of animals (*fig. 97*)

Poussin, Nicolas. French painter. Born in Villers (Les Andelys) in 1594, died in Rome in 1665. After training in Paris, Poussin went (1624) to Rome, where he worked in the studio of Domenichino and came under his influence. In the early 1630s he adopted a more romantic style under the influence of Titian but, during the later part of the 1630s, he moved towards a severer idiom, guided by antique sculpture and Raphael, which became in the 1640s and 1650s a high-water mark of French classicism. Almost all his mature works were painted for private patrons, often of an intellectual cast of mind. 1640–2 he returned to Paris (*figs. 153–9*)

Pozzo, Andrea del. Italian painter and architect. Born in Trent in 1642, died in Vienna in 1709. The most dazzling exponent of illusionist painting in the history of Italian baroque painting. In 1665 he entered the Jesuit order but continued to paint. After a successful career in Rome, he settled in Vienna in 1702 (*fig. 19*)

Rembrandt Harmenszoon van Rijn. Dutch painter, draughtsman and etcher. Born in Leyden in 1606, died in Amsterdam in 1669. One of the most important of seventeenth-century painters. Pupil of Pieter Lastman, who introduced him to the device of chiaroscuro, which had originated in Italy. This contrast of light and shadow became, under Rembrandt's hand, a unique medium of expression, full of compelling evocation. His range was remarkably wide; he produced religious and mythological scenes, landscapes, still-life and portraits, both single and group. His early manner (up to the 1640s) is characterized by careful attention to detail, but he developed in the 1640s a freer handling and richer mode of colouring. He was also a prodigious draughtsman (*figs. 104–11*)

Reni, Guido. Italian painter. Born in Calvenzano in 1575, died in Bologna in 1642. Important representative of Italian baroque painting; pupil of the Carracci academy. Painter of frescoes, mythological and religious pictures. He became a leading exponent of the emotional, Bolognese classical style (*fig. 11*)

Ribera, Jusepe de. Spanish painter. Born in Játiva in 1591, died in Naples in 1652. By 1616 he had settled in Naples, where he became the leading exponent of dramatic, Neapolitan Caravaggism. His career falls into three parts: up to the mid-1630s he stressed dark backgrounds, startling compositions, violent contrasts of light and shade, and a dry use of paint; c 1635–c 1640 he preferred softer colour, lighter backgrounds and ecstatic subjects; in the 1640s he blended the two manners into a rich and evocative style, looser and more liquid in handling, richer in colour and with an increased spiritualization of types (*figs. 24–7*)

Rigaud, Hyacinthe. French painter. Born in Perpignan in 1659, died in Paris in 1743. Important creator of court portraits during the reigns of Louis XIV and Louis XV. He portrayed Louis XIV in the large painting where Le Roi Soleil 'displays his leg'. Despite his refinement and virtuosity his paintings seem to be lacking in essential human significance (*fig. 175*)

Rizi (Ricci), Juan. Spanish painter. Born in Madrid in 1600, died in Monte Cassino in 1681. Painter of religious pictures. Was an apprentice of Mayno and was influenced by Velázquez. Became a Benedictine monk in 1670 (*fig. 49*)

Rubens, Peter Paul (Petrus Paulus). Flemish painter. Born in Siegen in 1577, died in Antwerp in 1640. The most outstanding representative of Flemish baroque painting worked in Italy, France, England and Spain. His style was moulded under many influences – antique sculpture, Raphael, Michelangelo, Titian, etc – and its forceful, rhetorical vigour was ideally suited to Catholic propaganda. He ran a large studio, which produced a steady stream of altar-pieces, Madonnas, mythological and allegorical subjects, landscapes and portraits, as well as decorative schemes, often worked up from the master's sketches, and re-touched by him at the end. His landscapes, though, are mostly autograph. He often employed specialists for such elements as flowers or still-life. He had a decisive influence on the course of seventeenth-century Flemish painting (*figs. 63–70*)

Ruysdael, Jacob van. Dutch landscape painter. Born in Haarlem c 1628, died there in 1682. Fine romantic landscape painter who is more famous today than his uncle Salomon. Salomon probably influenced Jacob, although the latter developed a more 'impetuous', more vigorous style, handing it down, in turn, to his equally well known pupil Hobbema (*figs. 100 and 101*)

Saenredam, Pieter. Dutch painter. Born in Assendelft in 1597, died in Haarlem in 1665. A pupil of F. P. de Grebber at Haarlem. He specialized in the painting of architecture, especially church interiors, which he reproduced (especially in his drawings) with great fidelity (*fig. 96*)

Saraceni, Carlo (Carlo Veneziano). Italian painter. Born in Venice in 1585, died there in 1620. At the age of seventeen he came to Rome and fell under the influence of Caravaggio, while the influence of Elsheimer can also be traced in his work. He learned to combine Caravaggio's strong realism with the more temperate colours so characteristic of his native town. He produced paintings in churches and palaces in Rome, Venice and other cities (*fig. 9*)

Savery, Roeland(t). Flemish painter. Born in Comtrai in 1576, died in Utrecht in 1639. Painter of landscapes and of biblical and mythological scenes. Court painter in Vienna and Prague (*fig. 78*)

Seghers, Hercules. Dutch painter and etcher. Born in Haarlem or Amsterdam c 1589/90, died in The Hague or in Amsterdam c 1638. 'A sombre, tragic figure' (Hoogstraten) who, nevertheless, was among the greatest Dutch landscape painters. A pupil of Gilles van Coninxloo, he was admired by Rembrandt, who owned eight of his landscapes, and was influenced by his style. He adopted fantastic mountainous motifs from his predecessors, but treated them in a more realistic, though often romantic way. He was a brilliant etcher (*figs. 82 and 83*)

Snyders, Frans. Flemish painter. Born in Antwerp in 1579, died there in

1657. Collaborator of Rubens. Painted mainly animal and flower pieces, all of which reveal the influence of Rubens (*fig. 79*)

Steen, Jan. Dutch painter. Born in Leyden *c* 1626, died there in 1679. Probably a pupil of his father-in-law, Jan van Goyen. He also studied with Adriaen van Ostade. He specialized in genre scenes, good-humoured records of peasant and middle-class life and mores in a vigorous, though carefully finished style. A few landscapes by him are known (*fig. 125*)

Streeck, Juriaen van. Dutch painter. Born in Amsterdam *c* 1632, died there in 1687. Important still-life and portrait painter. Characteristic of his art is the presentation of precious metals or vessels of Delft blue (*fig. 126*)

Tassel, Jean. French painter. Born *c* 1608. He studied with his father, Richard Tassel, and also under Jean Leclerc. He went to Rome in 1634 and was influenced by the Caravaggesque movement. Back in France, he worked mainly at Dijon and Langres, in an uneven style in which the influences of Reni, Veronese, Vouet, La Hyre and Rubens may be detected. He died in 1667 (*fig. 148*)

Teniers the Younger, David. Flemish painter. Born in Antwerp in 1610, died in Brussels in 1690. One of the most characteristic Flemish genre painters, he produced a long series of genre, landscapes, portraits and still-life. He specialized in low-life genre which he treated with a lively, commercial charm. Much ot his work ultimately stems from the Elder Brueghel (*figs. 74–6*)

Terborch, Gerard. Dutch genre painter. Born in Zwolle in 1617, died in Deventer in 1681. Pupil of Pieter de Molijn in Haarlem. He travelled in England, Italy, Germany, France and Spain. His early works are in the style of Codde, Duyster and other *corps de garde* painters, while in the 1640s he was producing small-scale portraits in a meticulous technique, which were the basis of the elegant interiors with figures on which his fame rests. He was specially famous for his treatment of satin (*figs. 91 and 92*)

Terbrugghen, Hendrick. Dutch painter. Born in Deventer in 1588 (?), died in Utrecht in 1629. Together with Gerard van Honthorst (Gherardo della Notte) and Barburen, he was responsible for introducing Caravaggio's style into Dutch painting. Terbrugghen was, like Honthorst, a pupil of Bloemaert, and after his work in Italy he became the outstanding representative of the School of Utrecht. He painted biblical scenes, mainly taken from the Old Testament, genre pieces and portraits in half length (*fig. 77*)

Testelin, Henri. French painter and writer on art. Born in Paris in 1616, died in The Hague in 1695. One of the founders of the Académie de Peinture (1648). As a Protestant he was forced to take refuge in Holland. Portrait painter (*fig. 176*)

Tour, Georges de la. French painter. Born in Vic-sur-Seille in 1593, died in Lunéville in 1652. Too little is known about the life of this great painter for us to be certain whether he ever stayed in Italy. At any rate, Caravaggio exercised his influence upon him, either by immediate relationship, through the medium of Leclerq, who had returned to France from Rome, or through the Dutchmen Honthorst and Terbrugghen. He found his own style, mainly in night scenes lit by a candle or a torch (*figs. 142–6*)

Tournier, Nicolas. French painter. Born in Toulouse in 1590, died in 1657. 1619–26 he was in Rome where he came under the influence of Caravaggio and his followers, whose idiom he imported to Toulouse (*fig. 170*)

Váldes Leal (Juan de Nisa). Spanish painter, sculptor, goldsmith and engraver. Born in Seville in 1622, died there in 1690. He was one of the founders of the Seville Academy in 1660, and was President 1663–6. He produced altar-pieces and large-scale religious paintings for churches and religious foundations (*figs. 46 and 47*)

Valentin de Boulogne. Franco-Italian painter. Born in Coulommiers *c* 1594. By 1614 he was in Rome, where he died in 1632. Painter of religious scenes and genre pieces, which reveal the influence of such followers of Caravaggio as Vouet and Manfredi (*fig. 169*)

Velázquez, Diego da Silva y. Spanish painter. Born in Seville in 1599, died in Madrid in 1660. After his apprenticeship with Herrera and Pacheco, he was appointed court painter at the age of twenty-four. His early works, especially the genre scenes, are cast in a strong Caravaggesque mould, but he developed in the late 1620s and 1630s a much less dramatic, lighter-toned style of direct painting, notable for its discreet mastery of optical effects, its subtle and beautiful colours, and its ability to convey an impartial sense of character. He specialized in portraits, usually of the King and Spanish Court, but he also painted religious and mythological scenes (*figs. 28–35*)

Velde, Adriaen van de. Dutch painter. Born in Amsterdam in 1636, died there in 1672. Well known painter of landscapes and of biblical and mythological scenes. Influenced at first by Potter, he later turned to a form of Italianizing landscape in the manner of Berchem (*fig. 121*)

Vermeer van Delft, Jan. Dutch painter. Born in Delft in 1632, died there in 1675. With Rembrandt and Hals, he is the most distinguished of seventeenth-century Dutch painters. Little is known about his life. It is supposed that he was an apprentice of Rembrandt's pupil Carel Fabritius. His great reputation rests on a small number of middle-class interiors with figures, akin to those de Hoogh, but distinguished by an exceptional feeling for composition and the fall of light. To the extent that he observed the optical effects of light empirically and accurately he is, like the young Corot, an important precursor of the Impressionists (*figs. 114–19*)

Vos, Paul de. Flemish painter. Born in Hulst *c* 1596, died in Antwerp in 1678. Painter of animal and hunting scenes under the influence of Rubens. His style was close to that of his brother-in-law, Frans Snyders (*fig. 54*)

Vouet, Simon. French painter, born in 1590 in Paris, where he died in 1649. 1614–27 he was in Italy, principally in Rome; he was influenced by Caravaggio but in the early 1620s evolved a more classical and decorative idiom in which influences from Lanfranco and Guercino, Guido Reni and Domenichino are apparent. Back in Paris, he ran an important and influential studio which was much occupied with decorative work; his pupils included the two Mignards, Le Sueur and Le Brun (*fig. 174*)

Zurbarán, Francisco de. Spanish painter. Born in Fuente de Cantos in 1598, died in Madrid in 1664. During his career as a painter he came under the influence of Herrera, Caravaggio and Murillo, but succeeded in attaining a form of expression entirely his own which endows his pictures sometimes with a transcendental quality. He stands far remote from Velázquez in spite of their friendship. He is the painter of Roman Catholic and mystical Spain of the seventeenth-century. He produced religious paintings almost exclusively (*figs. 39–45*)